SAPPHO

Complete Poems and Fragments

SAPPHO

Complete Poems and Fragments

Translated by
Stanley Lombardo

Introduction by
Pamela Gordon

Hackett Publishing Company, Inc.
Indianapolis/Cambridge

Printed in the United States of America

19 18 17 16 1 2 3 4 5 6 7

For further information, please address
Hackett Publishing Company, Inc.
P.O. Box 44937
Indianapolis, Indiana 46244-0937

www.hackettpublishing.com

Cover design by Brian Rak
Composition by William Hartman

Library of Congress Cataloging-in-Publication Data

Names: Sappho, author. | Lombardo, Stanley, 1943– translator.
Title: Complete poems and fragments / Sappho ;
translated by Stanley Lombardo ; introduction by Pamela Gordon.
Description: Indianapolis ; Cambridge : Hackett Publishing
Company, 2016.
Identifiers: LCCN 2015041308 | ISBN 9781624664687 (cloth)
| ISBN 9781624664670 (pbk.)
Subjects: LCSH: Sappho—Criticism and interpretation.
Classification: LCC PA4408.E5 L653 2016 | DDC 884/.01—dc23
LC record available at http://lccn.loc.gov/2015041308

The paper used in this publication meets the minimum requirements of American National Standard for Information Sciences—Permanence of Paper for Printed Library Materials, ANSI Z39.48–1984.

∞

Contents

For

Li & Mei
Lily & Madison
&
Bailey Mae

Introduction
Searching for Sappho

Sappho was a Greek poet who lived on the island of Lesbos in the late seventh and early sixth centuries B.C.E. But she is also a construct, a phantom, an icon. Writing about her is a hazardous enterprise. The surviving texts are few (two or three complete poems, plus the scattered remnants), and the legends are vast. With so few verses and so many myths to go on, a writer inevitably exposes more about her own context than she can reveal about Sappho's.

Even the textual tradition of Sappho's poems has mythic qualities. To start from what might have been the end, legend has it that the early church ordered Sappho's books to be burnt, and thus reduced us to eking out our text of Sappho from scraps and leavings. Whether or not deliberate book-burnings hastened the damage wrought by time and bad luck, the survival of the slender corpus as it exists today is as good a story. Roughly two-thirds of the verses that survive today were lost for over a millennium, to resurface only in the last years of the nineteenth and the first decades of the twentieth and twenty-first centuries. Some survived in improbable ways. Sappho's second fragment provides a striking example. Broken clay pots were often recycled into "scrap paper" in antiquity, and among the usual receipts and shopping lists, one occasionally finds an oddly enchanting message such as: "Leave the saw under the sill of the garden gate" (scratched on a potsherd found in Athens). But one particular broken pot delivers a message of a different order:

> . . . down from the mountain-top . . .
>
> and out of Crete, come to me here
> in your sacred precinct, to your grove
> of apple trees and your altars
> smoking with incense,

where cold water flows babbling
through the branches, the whole place
shadowed with roses . . .

This text, along with the rest of fragment 2, was lost until 1937, when the Italian scholar Medea Norsa published it, along with a photograph of the potsherd on which it was written. The text clearly represents the lyrics of a song to Aphrodite, the Greek goddess of erotic love (also called "Cypris," as at the end of this fragment). We know the fragment belongs to Sappho because almost every word matches what we know of Sappho's Aeolic Greek dialect, and because the text overlaps with three previously known snippets identified explicitly as Sappho's: one quoted in Athenaeus' *The Learned Banquet*, and two others in Hermogenes' *On Kinds of Style* (both Greek writers from the second-century C.E.). Like those quotations, the potsherd text was selected and copied at some remove from the poet's own world. The writing on the pottery scrap itself has since deteriorated, but the 1937 photograph reveals a graceful hand, in pen and ink. In many Greek-speaking areas, the usual way to write on a piece of pottery was to scratch the letters with a sharp tool, but pen and ink were the norm in Egypt. Thus, the potsherd comes to us not from Lesbos (or Mytilene, as Sappho's island is now called), but presumably from Egypt. The style of handwriting dates the text to somewhere around the third-century B.C.E., perhaps three or four hundred years after Sappho.

We cannot know how the lyrics of fragment 2 came to be written on a broken pot. Some scholars imagine a wistful lover wanting to have these words close at hand, as though they might charm an idyllic love scene into reality. Others posit more prosaic contexts: a scribe practicing the trade, or a student obediently responding to dictation. For the other fragments, the circumstances of survival are more transparent. Most of Sappho's extant poems come to us in one of two ways: either as centuries-old scraps of papyrus or parchment (ancient equivalents to paper), or as quotations in various books that were copied and passed along from era to era.

When ancient pieces of papyrus are fortuitously preserved, we usually end up with random snatches of discontinuous text, as in the beginning of fragment 21 in this edition:

lament
trembling

The circumstances of the survival of such shreds of text—and three twenty-first-century discoveries—will be discussed below. Quotations, on the other hand, are examples cited by ancient scholars who could not know that their essays and handbooks would outlive the bulk of Sappho's entire corpus. Several of the briefest quotations end with the words "and so on," as though any reader could be expected to know the full text. This type of fragment usually preserves at least a full phrase, as in fragment 52:

> I do not expect to graze the sky.

This verse has endured simply because a second-century C.E. scholar was interested in Sappho's unusual spelling of the Greek word for "sky." To cite another example: the rhetorician Hermogenes quotes "where cold water flows babbling / through the branches" (also in the potsherd fragment quoted above) as an example of a simple description that brings pleasure to the ear, just as beholding the beauty of the actual place would bring pleasure to the eye.

Until the end of the nineteenth century, such embedded quotations were the only known texts of Sappho. Fortunately, a few of them are just long enough to give us a glimpse of Sappho's genius. Poem 1 in this edition is cited in full by Dionysius of Halicarnassus, a Greek critic and historian who taught rhetoric in Rome in the first-century B.C.E. Praising the way the words are interwoven, Dionysius quotes poem 1 in his essay *On Literary Composition* as an example of "polished and exuberant" expression.

The other quotation of significant length is the almost complete Sappho 31, which comes to us from *On the Sublime*, a work on literary genius attributed to a shadowy first-century C.E. figure usually referred to as "Longinus." Longinus quotes fragment 31 as an example of brilliance in isolating and juxtaposing the symptoms of intense erotic desire. Longinus rightly admires how the poem describes the lover's heightened awareness of the convergence (*synodos*) of incongruous emotions. But the poem is also remarkable for the way it captures the triangle: the beloved, the man who has her attention, and the onlooker who possesses only her own overwhelming desire. As Anne Carson writes, the otherwise unidentified man and two women "are three points of transformation on a circuit of possible relationship, electrified by desire so that they touch not touching" (*Eros the Bittersweet* 16).

The contexts of the shorter embedded fragments are seldom revealing or illuminating, but lines cited for the most mundane of purposes have a way of leaping out at the reader and asserting their presence. Some of the most suggestive short fragments come from Apollonius Dyscolus' work *On Pronouns*, a technical treatise on the forms and uses of pronouns in the various Greek dialects. Apollonius focuses on Sappho's archaic Lesbian-Aeolic spellings of words like "you" and "me," but this interest leads him inadvertently to preserve:

> Towards you, lovely ones, my thoughts
> never change.
> (fr. 41)

Elsewhere in the same treatise, he records:

> Or you love someone else more
> (fr. 129ii)

Apollonius Dyscolus also gives us the minimalist but pleasing:

> as long as you are willing
> (fr. 45)

A discussion of place names by the first-century B.C.E. geographer Strabo yields:

> you either Cyprus or Paphos or Panormos
> (fr. 35)

Here the place names are rich with associations. There was a cult to Aphrodite at Paphos (on the island Cyprus), and Panormus—now Palermo—was a new Phoenician city on Sicily (though some scholars place it, too, on Cyprus). From the perspective of an archaic Greek islander, Cyprus and Sicily were on opposite ends of the earth. What verb is missing? Should we supply "invokes you," "detains you," or "calls you"? Could there be a tone of loss or impatience? Has a mortal abandoned a lover, or has Aphrodite deserted Sappho? Or, is a chorus of worshippers calling for Aphrodite's return to a temple on Lesbos?

The many editions and translations of Sappho that appeared during the nineteenth-century revival of Sappho were based exclusively on such quotations. But, in the last years of the nineteenth century, the corpus of Sappho's poems suddenly began to grow. The first new fragments were discovered, along with papyrus scraps of receipts, leases, letters, and an array of great literary works in the Roman-era trash heaps of an Egyptian town called Oxyrhynchus. Tattered Greek texts on papyrus (the usual writing material for literature) probably ended up frequently in ancient landfills elsewhere. But only in the dry climate of Oxyrhynchus were large quantities of legible papyri preserved in this manner, and even in Oxyrhynchus, the oldest layers of rubbish reside below the water table and thus do not yield any texts. Some of the Oxyrhynchus papyri contain nearly complete poems, like the justly famous fragment 16i, which opens with:

> Some say an army on horseback, some say on foot,
> and some say ships are the most beautiful things
> on this black earth, but I say
> it is whatever you love.

But others are sadly full of holes:

> proceed
> so we may see
>
> Lady Dawn
> her golden arms
>
> fate
> (fr. 6)

A few other Sappho texts on papyrus or parchment were also discovered at other sites in Egypt, and many fragments of Sappho continued to emerge from the excavations at Oxyrhynchus between 1897 and 1934 (some published as late as 1951). But, to the surprise of readers and scholars around the world, a papyrus fragment containing almost a full poem by Sappho was revealed in 2004 (poem 58, "The Tithonus Poem" or "Sappho on Old Age"), followed in 2014 by two more relatively well-preserved texts, as well as a new minor fragment and a few slender supplements to fragments 5, 9, 16, 17, and possibly 18. These twenty-first-century discoveries were extracted from the remains of objects fabricated from *cartonnage*, an Egyptian material similar to papier-mâché, and recently purchased on the antiquities market. Poem 58 was uncovered at the University of Cologne (Universität zu Köln) on Egyptian mummy cartonnage. The two others were recovered by a private owner from similarly recycled papyrus (possibly a book binding rather than funerary cartonnage, since it was not plastered or painted).

The new poem 58 (labeled 58i in this edition) overlaps considerably with what used to be the poorly preserved "fragment 58," a shattered song that was missing the first words of almost every line. Suddenly, we seem to have everything except several syllables from the beginnings of the first two lines. For some scholars, it is now clear that the poem opens with the singer exhorting a group of girls (perhaps a chorus for a religious festival, or perhaps a more generalized implied audience) to devote themselves to music and dance ("the Muses' gifts"), the implication being that these arts belong to youth, a stage the singer has long passed. But, according to an interpretation that proposes that the first line should begin with something such as "I bring" rather than "devote yourselves," the singer is asserting that she—despite her age—retains full possession of the music. She concedes that dancing (but not the art of song) must be left to the young. To keep interpretation open, this edition preserves the fractured state of the first four lines, while accepting the nearly certain addition of the word "Muses":

violet-robed Muses' gifts, girls,
the clear-toned, melodious lyre.

my skin once soft, but age now
my black hair has become

My heart is heavy, and my knees will not carry me,
though once they were light as a fawn's in the dance.

The singer (perhaps to be understood as Sappho) laments her old age, but recognizes that physical decline was the stark reality even for the mythological Tithonus, the beautiful human boy who was carried off by the Dawn goddess, to be her lover:

> They always said rose-armed Dawn loved Tithonus
> and took him away, a beautiful young boy,
>
> to the edge of the world. But in time grey old age
> seized him, even though he slept with an immortal.

Sappho may have expected her audience to know the story as told in the Homeric *Hymn to Aphrodite*, where Aphrodite says that Dawn had exacted from the gods the promise of immortality for Tithonus, but had forgotten to ask for his eternal youth.

The discovery of the new papyrus for poem 58i thickens the plot of the story of the survival of Sappho's lyrics. Classical scholarship often focuses on reconstructing the exact words of an ancient poet and the order of the poems as they appeared in the standard ancient edition. But the two papyri that preserve poem 58 (one preserving 58i and the other preserving that text plus 58ii) also transmit completely different texts for the preceding poem. To mark the discrepancy, this edition labels these fragmentary texts Papyrus Oxyrhynchus 1787 and Papyrus Köln inv. 21351 & 21376. The new Köln papyrus clearly marks the four lines about Tithonus (quoted above) as the poem's ending, whereas the fragmentary version of 58 transmitted by the previously discovered Oxyrhynchus papyrus continues for four more lines:

> thinks
> might send with
>
> But I love delicacy   and this has won for me
> radiant passion and the beauty of the sun.

Such an ending would fill out the second interpretation mentioned above: in full control of her artistic powers and sensibilities, our aging singer has achieved an eminence approaching the immortal. The Köln papyrus—now our earliest Sappho fragment—is older by about 500 years, so many scholars regard the shorter poem as the more authentic version. But, it is possible that Sappho herself performed more than one version of this song, and we may wonder whether we should regard any of her surviving poems as definitive texts.

In 2014, just when scholars had become accustomed to referring to the Köln version of poem 58 as "the new Sappho," two especially significant fragmentary texts appeared together on the same papyrus (usually now referred to as the Brothers poem and the Cypris poem). The attribution to Sappho is assured by meter, dialect, a few lines that overlap with previously discovered papyri, and by some references to the names of Sappho's brothers (known from other texts). The Brothers poem (here labeled as Papyrus Sappho Obbink) is a previously unknown poem that we have placed in this edition before fragment 5, roughly where the new papyrus seems to place it. It is tempting to interpret this new poem in the light of a story about Sappho's brother Charaxus, as recounted by the fifth-century B.C.E. writer Herodotus. According to this tale, Charaxus (reputedly a wine merchant) sailed home to Lesbos from Egypt after ransoming a courtesan there "for a great sum of money" (Herodotus 2.135). Herodotus adds that Sappho reviled Charaxus in a poem, but the surviving lines of the Brothers poem lack abusive language, and Herodotus may have had another poem in mind.

We print the Cypris poem as fragment 26 in this edition because it overlaps with the more tenuous fragment 26 that was discovered a century earlier in Oxyrhynchus. This poem addressed to Aphrodite resonates with poem 1, where Aphrodite promises a spurned lover that the beloved will in turn be love-struck "though unwilling." The Cypris poem may involve a story of desperate erotic desire from the point of view of an unwilling but painfully passionate lover:

> How could one not constantly be sick,
> Lady Cypris, if you are not her friend,
> and when she yearns to conceal her passion
> you don't hold her back?
> (fr. 26)

Although the papyri have more than tripled the number of surviving lines of Sappho's poetry, we still possess only a tiny fraction of the original corpus. Half a millennium after her death, the great library at Alexandria housed a collection of Sappho's poems that consisted of at least eight papyrus rolls, or books. The first-century B.C.E. poet Tullius Laurea—who wrote an epigram in Sappho's voice—counted nine books, but perhaps there was more than one edition in circulation among Roman readers. It is unlikely that Sappho ever conceived of a "complete works," but the number nine had particular resonances and may thus owe something to Sappho's legendary fame. Later generations counted Sappho as the lone woman among the nine Greek lyric poets, and Tullius Laurea suggests that there was a book of Sappho for each of the muses, those goddess-daughters of Zeus (traditionally nine in number) who inspire all poetic voices. An epigram attributed to Plato named Sappho herself as the tenth muse (these epigrams are included in this volume).

While British and European archaeologists were discovering new texts by Sappho in Egypt, various women artists were attempting a different sort of Sapphic recovery. Some reinvented Sappho's Lesbos in Paris, but others tried to recuperate a lost Lesbian heritage for women writers by sailing to the island of Lesbos itself. The writers Natalie Barney and Renée Vivien, for example, traveled together to Lesbos via Constantinople in 1904 and set up house there. Although Barney and Vivien conceptualized Sappho in diverse ways, both regarded her as a model for poetic as well as erotic expression, and they apparently hoped to found an island community of lesbian poets. Vivien spent several seasons in Lesbos, but plans for a modern Sapphic community seem to have faded out even before Vivien's premature death in 1909. Other artists who sailed to Lesbos in the first decades of the century include the American poet H.D. (a.k.a. Hilda Doolittle), whose modernist work was heavily influenced by Sappho's fragments. In the 1970s, Monique Wittig proposed a metaphorical escape to Mytilene: ". . . farewell black continent of misery and suffering farewell ancient cities we are embarking for the shining radiant isles for the green Cytheras for the dark and gilded Lesbos" (*The Lesbian Body* 26).

Travel to Sappho's island is considerably easier now than it was a century ago. Mytilene remains beautiful, though today's pilgrims may be as disenchanted by the proliferation of boutique and resort hotels as Natalie Barney and Renée Vivien apparently were by the loud music blaring in the harbor of Mytilene when they arrived in 1904. Although traveling to Lesbos gives Sappho's readers an idea of the sea, olive trees, vineyards, and the bright Aegean light that surrounded the poet, we are still over two and a half millennia away when we get there. It is also unlikely—though still possible—that new fragments of Sappho's poems will regularly emerge from the sands of Egypt, from museum storerooms or from small objects purchased at auction. But rather than focusing on the loss and the distance, the reader of Sappho can develop fruitful approaches to the surviving poems.

Reading among the Ruins

First, it is useful to think about different modes of reading a poem and about the various preconceptions and attitudes of the reader. Some of us, picking up a text of Sappho for the first time, might be struck by the immediacy of the emotions expressed in the poems, and we might read as though we were gaining direct access to Sappho, despite the distance in centuries and cultures. If we read that way (whether in Greek or in translation), all the books and scholarly articles about Sappho and her culture may seem like an encumbrance that threatens to get between us and the Sapphic voice. An extensive bibliography seldom satisfies a longing to speak with the dead. But many of the traditional scholarly works in fact represent another way of trying to get closer to Sappho. The whole point of much nineteenth- and early twentieth-century classical scholarship on Sappho was to reconstruct the poet's world so as to transport the scholar to Sappho's circle as she sang her songs. Thus, the novice reader of Sappho who reads with her heart has something in common with Ulrich von Wilamowitz, the famous nineteenth-century German classical scholar who devoted so many years to the archaic Greek poets. Wilamowitz had a passionate faith in classics as a science, and he believed that painstaking scholarly work would result in accurate accounts of the lives and minds of the Greek poets.

Perhaps the most rewarding way to read Sappho is by embracing a position somewhere between two extremes: read with one's own desires and interests in the open, but keep one foot in Wilamowitz's study. It is helpful to recognize the hazards of both modes of reading, to remember what those two poles might have in common and to be open to the possibility of entirely different approaches. One approach is to read an individual fragment as though we were reading a note in a bottle washed up by the tide. Each fragment comes to us against the odds and across the centuries, and none arrives with any original instructions about context or meaning. All we know is that the sender is Sappho (though, occasionally, we are not even sure of that), and some of us are certain that we are the right recipient. It can help to remember that most of the fragments we have were reattached to the other collected remnants of Sappho's work less than a century ago. It can be useful to know that fragment 2, for example, had no readers for centuries, until its message miraculously arrived in modern Europe.

One reason it is instructive to think of a fragment as an isolated note in a bottle is that we never have a precise archaic context in which to reinsert any particular fragment or poem. Early twentieth-century women writers who formed Sapphic writing circles were inspired by an interpretation of the poems to which many—though not all—scholars of ancient Greek would lend their support: Sappho does seem to have composed her songs within a community of girls and women, and yet our reconstructions of that circle are based primarily on our readings of the fragments themselves. So little is certain, and scholarly consensus often turns out to be built on shifting foundations. In fact, we cannot prove definitively that there was any type of group— private, religious, ceremonial, aristocratic, or otherwise—that gathered around Sappho. There are no biographies of Sappho except the various biographies that other readers have constructed from the fragments and legends. There is no detailed history of archaic Lesbos. If musical scores for the poems ever existed, they are irrevocably lost. In many ways, the generation of Wilamowitz was far too optimistic about how much we can know.

The existing biographies are especially suspect. Generations of readers have assumed that some bare "facts" are unassailable, e.g., that Sappho had a husband named Kerkylas, a daughter named Kleis, and three brothers: Charaxus, Eurygius, and Larichus. The notorious problem with the alleged husband is that his name is probably a joke, as Wilamowitz noticed (*Sappho und Simonides* 24). The ultimate source of the ancient encyclopedia that names Kerkylas specifies that he came from Andros (an actual Greek island). Since Kerkylas sounds a lot like a Greek word for "tail" or "penis" (*kerkos*), and since Andros is also the Greek word for "man," the supposed facts about Sappho's husband were probably the punning inventions of a Greek comic poet. The names for the brothers and daughter do not raise similar suspicions, but Kleis and Sappho's brothers probably made their way into the biographical tradition directly from the poems. (In their zeal to reconstruct the lives of great artists, ancient biographers often mistook fictional characters for real-life people.) In fragment 132, the poet's voice declares:

> I have a beautiful child who looks like
> golden flowers, my beloved Kleis,
> whom I would not trade for all Lydia
> or for lovely . . .

Even if we take this fragment as a factual statement by the historical "Sappho" (not necessarily a good way to read a poem), there is an additional problem with the historicity of Kleis. In recent decades, scholars have noticed that Sappho's word for "child" (*pais*) does not necessarily mean "daughter" or "offspring." Instead, it is a word with a wide range that can refer to any young person, male or female. In addition to being a familiar word for a slave (of any age), it was a common word for a favorite: a boyfriend or a girlfriend. In this poem, the grammatical gender of the Greek adjectives makes clear that Kleis is female. But, she may be a companion rather than a daughter.

It would be misleading, however, to claim that every surviving text of Sappho is an entirely disembodied voice. Unlike a simple note in a bottle, each fragment comes from a song that resonates with other surviving songs and poems from the Greek islands and cities. The projection of a distinct personal voice is characteristic of the work of Sappho and the other "lyric" poets (so named because their songs were accompanied by a stringed instrument we usually refer to as a lyre). But if we read as though a fragment represents Sappho's soul laid bare on the page, we may mistake the words of a character within a song for the expression of Sappho's own desires (even if the character calls herself "Sappho"). Or, we may mistake a brilliant work of art for a personal, private outpouring. Here it is useful to recognize that modern assumptions about personal poetry are especially problematic when applied to antiquity. Some classical scholars would go so far as to say that all ancient poetry is public by nature and that there is no such thing as a private voice in archaic Greek texts. Others counter, however, that Sappho—the only significant archaic woman's voice we have—is the great exception. At first reading, we may take her first-person assertions as straightforward confessions from "the real Sappho," but an awareness of other poetry from Sappho's era brings a more informed response to that poetic "I." The seventh-century Greek poet Archilochus, for example, sounds like an outrageously vengeful individual to readers unaware of the conventions of abuse poetry. Archilochus' personal rage seems to find analogues in the passionate agony of Sappho's compatriot Alcaeus and in Sappho's intense desire. But, when we read them together, we see that some degree of creative fiction is involved. This does not mean that Sappho's tone is artificial or insincere when she writes:

> Truly I wish I were dead.
> She was weeping when she left me . . .
> (fr. 94)

To the contrary, the first-person declaration pulls us into the poet's orbit and conjures up an intimate scene that is more expansive than a page literally dropped from someone's diary. Sappho even invites us to "believe in" her, for her love poems are not anonymous, but include characters who address a lover named "Sappho" within the poems. Thus, fragment 94 continues:

> She was weeping when she left me,
>
> and said many things to me, and said this:
> "How much we have suffered, Sappho.
> Truly, I do not want to leave you."

That we are not simply overhearing actual conversations between historical people becomes even clearer when we consider a poem in which Aphrodite herself addresses Sappho. This is poem 1, in which Sappho calls upon the goddess:

> Mind shimmering, deathless Aphrodite,
> child of Zeus, weaver of wiles,
> I beg you, do not crush my spirit
> with anguish, Lady,
>
> but come here now . . .

In this poem, Sappho asserts that she has reason to expect the goddess to appear, for she has descended to Sappho from heaven before, drawn in her chariot "through the middle air"— by sparrows:

> and then you were with me, a smile
> playing about your immortal lips
> as you asked what was it this time, why was I
> calling you again,

The wonderful irony here is that Sappho's love goddess is echoing the conventional language of Greek love poetry. As readers of the full range of Greek lyric know, the question "What or who is it this time?" (assigned thrice to Aphrodite in this poem) employs a Greek adverb that has a special resonance for lovers. This poignant and not-quite-translatable adverb (*deute*; "again," "this time," "once more") appears with remarkable frequency in Greek love poetry. As an article by Sarah Mace points out, we have this adverb in a very particular formula in several poems by four different archaic poets ("Amour, Encore! The Development of δηὖτε in Archaic Lyric" 335). Seven of those poems begin with the same three words: *Eros deute me* (Eros, once more . . . me). Eros, whence we get our word *erotic*, is Desire personified, and a distant relative of his Roman semi-equivalent, Cupid. He is a companion to Aphrodite and is often described as her divine son, equipped with weapons and wings. In the poems in the "Eros, once more . . ." series, and in Greek poetry in general, Eros is a serious force to be reckoned with. Recognizing something so simple as a repeated three-word formula gives us a glimpse of an ancient context something like an ongoing poetry slam in which the archaic poets competed to describe Eros adequately and to produce the best image to depict his attack. Thus, a sixth-century poet named Anacreon attempted to trounce his predecessors by delivering: "With a huge hammer Eros this time has struck me like a blacksmith and plunged me in an icy torrent" (Denys Page, *Poetae Melici Graeci* 413). In Sappho's own direct engagement with this tradition, Eros is both more seductive and more subtly distressing:

> Eros once more, limbslackener, makes me shudder,
> sweetbitter, irresistible, creeping thing
> (fr. 130)

Other poets applied the adjective "limbslackener" (*lusimeles*) to Eros, Sleep, Death, sickness, and wine; but "sweetbitter" (*glukupikron*) is apparently Sappho's own coinage. As Anne Carson suggests, here the word *deute* (translated in this fragment as "once more") marks both the startled widening of the eyes and the immediate narrowing as one thinks, "Oh, this again." To quote Carson, the word *deute* appears "like one long, rather wild sigh at the beginning of the poem, as the lover perceives her attacker and understands that it is (oh no!) already too late (not again!) to avoid desire" (*Eros the Bittersweet* 119).

To return to Sappho poem 1: By attributing the love poets' shared language to the love goddess herself, Sappho brings a new twist to the tradition. An awareness of that twist helps bring into focus Sappho's treatments of Eros and Aphrodite. By echoing the language of the human poets, Aphrodite is simultaneously siding with Sappho and taunting her with her own words. Or, does Sappho have such a tight connection to Aphrodite that the goddess competes with her to pin down the laws of desire? Elsewhere, we find the lone line: "I really talked with you in a dream, / Cyprogeneia" (fr. 134; Cyprogeneia, like Cypris, being a name for Aphrodite). Looking to other fragments, one hears both the confidence in Sappho's voice as she sings: "come to me here" (fr. 2), and the risk involved: "do not crush my spirit / with anguish" (poem 1). The danger of having Aphrodite against one is also apparent in the fragment that pleads: "O Cypris, may Dorikha find you / most bitter" (fr. 15). Although the text is uncertain, a glimmer of Aphrodite's sinister power may also shine through the damaged papyrus in fragment 5: "but you, Cypris, / disposing of the evil woman. . .". An indication of the varied meanings and powers of Aphrodite is evident too in the array of names with which Sappho addresses her: "Aphrodite," "child of Zeus," "weaver of wiles," "Lady," "Cypris," "Cyprogeneia," "Cytherea." Aphrodite's companion Eros also comes in many guises. We have already seen that he is "sweetbitter," "irresistible," and "creeping." A second-century C.E. scholar named Pollux tells us that in another of Sappho's lost poems, Eros arrives from heaven wearing a purple mantle. Also in the second century, a public lecturer named Maximus of Tyre quotes this Sapphic fragment:

> Eros has shaken my mind,
> wind swooping down the mountain on oaks.
> (fr. 47)

At the same point in that lecture (*Orations* 18.9), Maximus of Tyre gives us a glimpse of another side of Sappho's Eros by mentioning that Socrates calls Eros a "sophist" (a sort of itinerant professor highly criticized by Plato's Socrates) and Sappho calls him a *mythoplokos*, a "word-weaver" (fr. 188). The combined reference to Socrates and Sappho gives us a notion of Sappho's reputation for wisdom and her iconic status, but significant too is the fact that both authorities are calling Eros "a talker." Socrates' label for Eros implies that Desire traffics in verbal ploys and persuasion (and perhaps false advertising), but Sappho's name for Eros stresses the attractiveness of his stories. By calling Desire *mythoplokos*, Sappho reminds us how love needs a narrative and the lover needs an imagination. Sappho's name for Eros, the "word-weaver," also points to one of the most essential qualities of Sappho's own lyrics. The sounds and shapes of her verses are inimitable, but often, it is the sheer strength of narrative that comes through on the most fragile of fragments. Fragment 44i, which describes in intricate detail the marriage of Hector and Andromache, is the only fragment that gives us an idea of Sappho's sustained handling of a complex narrative. But, even in the shortest fragments, Sappho supplies us with the verbal images that have fed the imaginations of Sappho's readers: Anactoria's way of walking, the treachery of Atthis, the woman who rivals Helen, the man "like a god" impassively listening to a voice that is nearly killing the other listener.

In some eras of Sappho's varied afterlife, readers and scholars and novelists have wanted to shape Sappho's fragments into a single connected narrative. Often, the result has been a different and less-compelling sort of storytelling, with Sappho losing one lover after another and finally leaping to her death from the cliffs of Leucas. Or, there is the scholarly feat of bundling everything together into one unified narrative in which Sappho is a teacher who sends successive generations of lovely girls off to marriage. There is already a spark of this tradition in the works of the Roman poet Ovid (particularly *Heroides* 15, included in this volume), but its modern reincarnation began with Wilamowitz and an earlier scholar named Welcker. Notoriously, Wilamowitz brought even fragment 31 into this scheme: the sweetly talking girl as the bride, the godlike man as the groom, and Sappho as the stricken wedding singer (*Sappho und Simonides* 58).

Better to abandon the tangled mass of biography and return to the idea of the isolated message. We might miss the poem if we focus on constructing a life of Sappho in which she figures as a victim of unrequited love. Instead of trying to weave the fragments too closely together, why not take each one as it comes, remembering that a poem can resonate with other poems without becoming an entry in a single narrative? We might understand loss and absence, not as the tragic patterns of Sappho's own life, but as qualities inherent to her depiction of Eros. We might consider that love is like Sappho's apple:

> Like the sweet apple reddening on the topmost branch,
> the topmost apple on the tip of the branch, and the pickers
> forgot it,
> well, no, they didn't forget, they just couldn't reach it . . .
> (fr. 105i)

The Heavy Graeco-Asiatic Sunlight

Lesbos is closer to Asia Minor (equivalent to modern Turkey from the Aegean to the Euphrates) than it is to mainland Greece. In fact, Sappho's material world may have been less Greek than we sometimes imagine: In recent years, archaeologists have discovered that the architecture, pottery, and burial practices of archaic Lesbos may have more in common with the vestiges of ancient non-Greek cultures to the east than they do with the Greek cities to the west. Writing in the early twentieth century, H.D. extolled what she regarded as Sappho's quintessentially Dorian Greek qualities, but acknowledged a "heavy Graeco-Asiatic sunlight" ("The Wise Sappho" 63) and aspects that many scholars still count among the signs of Sappho's Asiatic orientation: incense, spices, lush detail, "a tint of rich colour . . . violets, purple woof of cloth, scarlet garments, dyed fastening of a sandal, the lurid, crushed and perished hyacinth, stains on cloth and flesh and parchment" ("The Wise Sappho" 57).

Particularly relevant here are Sappho's references to the Lydians, who controlled an empire that stretched across Asia Minor. A quotation included in an ancient scholarly comment (in the margins of a play by Aristophanes) on the superiority of Lydian dyes records:

sandals
of fine Lydian make, straps rainbow-dyed,
covered her feet
(fr. 39)

Part of one of the fragments refers to a mother's recollection of prized purple headbands from her youth, and also to "an embroidered headband/ from Sardis" (a Lydian city, now Turkish *Sart*). But now, the eastern product is inaccessible:

But, Kleis, I don't know where to get
an embroidered headband for you.
(fr. 98)

We cannot know whether Lesbos is the setting of this poem or whether we are to imagine the speaker in the west—perhaps in Sicily, where Sappho spent some time in exile (according to a Greek chronological inscription known as the Parian marble). Elsewhere, exotic fabric appears in a fragment that also mentions a Hellenized city on the coast of Asia Minor:

> and handkerchiefs . . . purple, scented
> from Phocaea
> expensive gifts
> (fr. 101)

To some scholars, Eastern motifs and the influence of Vedic Sanskrit poetic structures and patterns on Greek poetry are more palpable in Sappho's verses than in other Greek poetry, including the songs of Sappho's contemporary and Lesbian compatriot Alcaeus. In Sappho's song about Hector and Andromache (fr. 44i), the castanets and "myrrh and cassia and frankincense" are contemporary elements not associated with Troy in Homer. Furthermore, the Greeks considered their *barbiton* (the lyre-like instrument that Sappho likely played) to be an Eastern import. Also evocative of Eastern connections are Sappho's mention of "Delicate Adonis" (fr. 140), the young lover of Aphrodite whom the Greeks associated with the East. Perhaps similarly evocative are her frequent allusions to the goddess Dawn, who rises in the east and whose Eastern counterpart appears in Vedic hymns to the immortal goddess of the dawn (e.g., poem 58i and fr. 123), though songs about the non-Greek goddess of the dawn seem to include no counterpart to Dawn's mortal Tithonus (mentioned in poem 58i).

But Eastern influences appear throughout Greek culture. Here I note that in his ground-breaking work on Asiatic elements in Greek poetry and myth, M. L. West describes Eastern influences not only upon Sappho, but upon Greek literature by Aeschylus, Hesiod, and Homer, and, more generally, upon Greek prayer, religion, and mythology. Moreover, it is salutary to ask whether Sappho's sense of the Asiatic is as shaped by Greek views of the East as by her geographic proximity to Lydian culture. Eastern luxury items played an important role in Greek aristocratic elite lifestyles, and a Lydian headband and "an abundance of purple" are coveted items also in a poem from far away Sparta (Alcman's *Partheneion*, roughly contemporary with Sappho). Later, for the fifth-century Greek storyteller and historian who most famously delineated the stark antitheses between Greeks and non-Greeks, it was fundamental that Persians have extravagant clothing, that "the remotest parts of the world have the finest products" and that Arabia has a "godlike" fragrance (Herodotus, *Histories* 3.108 and 112). Modern orientalism and misogyny, and homophobia—not to mention the fragmentary nature of the texts or the lack of historical information—are not the only obstacles. Much of the difficulty stems from the fact that desire itself has no stable, cross-cultural value. Erotic desire may seem universal and timeless, but its shapes and their implications vary wildly from culture to culture, from language to language, from person to person. Few things are more culturally contingent than love and sex.

An obvious problem with naming Sappho a "lesbian" is that the ancient Greeks seem generally not to have thought about desire in terms of sexual orientation. A seventh-century Greek might assume that erotic desire takes many forms, but it is unlikely a Greek thought in terms of fixed categories that can be neatly translated into modern terms such as "lesbian," "bisexual," or "heterosexual." Thus, it is not surprising that some of Sappho's lyrics are ambiguous about the gender of the object of desire; it is also not surprising that the ambiguity sometimes lurks quietly behind the verses. Fragment 102, for example, seems clear-cut in English:

> Sweet mother, I can no longer work the loom.
> Slender Aphrodite has made me fall in love with a boy.

The word translated here as "boy" (*pais*) is likely to mean just that: a young male object of desire. But although *pais* is a very common word for "boy," it appears here with no gender-specific article or adjective. Thus, it is just possible that Sappho's original poem was not so specific: our distracting boy might be a girl. Elsewhere, we find similarly remarkable abstraction. Particular objects of desire—and the response to the beloved's distinct and individual qualities—emerge from Sappho's fragments with clarity and precision. When Sappho generalizes, however, the gender of the beloved disappears: "but I say / it is whatever you love" (fr. 16i).

When we move beyond modern preoccupations with sexual preference or orientation, the issues become more complicated. Readers in search of evidence for a female sexuality that differs radically from men's sexuality in antiquity have often turned to Sappho, and many scholars believe that Sappho's fragments do indeed view desire from a distinctly female angle (see, in particular, Jane Snyder 1997 and the essays by Ellen Greene, Marilyn Skinner, Eva Stehle, and Jack Winkler collected in Greene's *Reading Sappho*, 1996). Some have claimed that Sappho presents an erotics of reciprocity and mutuality that stands in stark contrast to other archaic poets' themes of masculine pursuit and feminine submission. Others have asserted that Sappho's poetry describes a community far removed from the male-centered, competitive world of archaic Greece. For many contemporary readers, such interpretations of Sapphic desire are essential to an understanding of Sappho as a poet of lesbian desire.

Poem 1, for instance, has often been described as an example of mutual passion. There, Aphrodite responds to the plea for help by assuring her that the beloved will soon become the lover:

> "Whom now
> should I persuade to love you? Who is
> wronging you, Sappho?
>
> "She may run now, but she'll be chasing soon.
> She may spurn gifts, but soon she'll be giving.

Where some readers see reciprocity, however, others see a desire for vengeance. The latter interpretation stresses the import of Aphrodite's next words:

> She may not love now, but she'll love soon,
> even unwilling."

In this reading, the last line of the poem ("Fight for me, Goddess") further links Sappho with the male lyric poets, who commonly describe love as military conquest. We can even go one step further and read the prayer to Aphrodite as a plea for justice (as does Anne Carson in her essay, "The Justice of Aphrodite in Sappho 1"). In this reading, Aphrodite is not promising reconciliation with the fleeing beloved. Rather, she is assuring the plaintiff that this unresponsive object of desire will soon suffer a similar plight. She too will fall in love, and she will find out how it feels to be spurned.

Readers who agree that some of the fragments describe an agonistic view of love need not abandon the search for a poetics of lesbian desire. A position articulated by the poet H.D. provides a case in point. H.D. celebrated Sappho's departures from heterosexual norms as H.D. knew them, but in her reading of the fragments, she did not find mutuality, equality, and reciprocity. Instead, H.D. valued Sappho's arrogance. For her, Sappho was: "Indifferent—full of caprice—full of

Margaret Williamson, *Sappho's Immortal Daughters* (Harvard University Press, 1995). Introductory studies focusing on the concept that desire and gender are performed and constructed (rather than universal or innate) include Page duBois's introduction to *Sappho Is Burning* and Thomas K. Hubbard, *A Companion to Greek and Roman Sexualities* (Wiley-Blackwell, 2014). Although they do not treat Sappho extensively, Kenneth Dover, *Greek Homosexuality* (Harvard University Press, 1978), and David Halperin, *One Hundred Years of Homosexuality* (Routledge, 1990), are still relevant.

Discussions of the possible contexts of Sappho's poetry in her own era include: Claude Calame, *Choruses of Young Women in Ancient Greece: Their Morphology, Religious Role, and Social Functions* (translated by Derek Collins and Janice Orion, Rowman & Littlefield, 2001); Franco Ferrari, *Sappho's Gift: The Poet and Her Community* (translated by Benjamin Acosta-Hughes and Lucia Prauscello, University of Michigan, 2010); Judith P. Hallett's article in Greene's *Reading Sappho*; and Eva Stehle, *Performance and Gender in Ancient Greece: Nondramatic Poetry in Its Setting* (Princeton University Press, 1997). Holt Parker offers a strong critique of the tradition of viewing Sappho as a teacher of young girls in "Sappho Schoolmistress" in Greene's *Re-Reading Sappho* (University of California Press, 1996).

Asiatic influences on Sappho are treated by Page duBois, *Out of Athens: The New Ancient Greeks* (Harvard University Press, 2010), and M. L. West, *The East Face of Helicon: West Asiatic Elements in Greek Poetry* (Oxford University Press, 1997). Archaeology is treated in the scholarly survey by Nigel Spencer, "Early Lesbos between East and West: A 'Grey Area' of Aegean Archaeology" (*The Annual of the British School at Athens*, 1995).

On responses to Sappho in later eras (ranging from antiquity through the twentieth century), see Diana Collecott, *H.D. and Sapphic Modernism 1910–1950* (Cambridge University Press, 2008); Joan DeJean, *Fictions of Sappho* (University of Chicago Press, 1989); Ellen Greene's *Re-Reading Sappho*; Yopie Prins, *Victorian Sappho* (Princeton University Press, 1999); Margaret Reynolds, *The Sappho History* (Palgrave Macmillan, 2003); and Dimitrios Yatromanolakis, *Sappho in the Making: The Early Reception* (Harvard University Press, 2007), which includes photographs of representations of Sappho on ancient Greek pottery.

Modern literary works include: H.D, *Notes on Thought and Vision & the Wise Sappho* (written around 1920, but first published by City Lights Books, 1982); Peter Green, *The Laughter of Aphrodite: A Novel about*

Sappho of Lesbos (University of California Press 1965, 1993); Erica Jong, *Sappho's Leap* (Norton, 2003); the many poems and libretti collected in Margaret Reynolds, *The Sappho Companion* (Palgrave, 2000); Marguerite Yourcenar, *Fires* (translated by Dorie Katz, Farrar Straus Giroux, 1981). For operas, see Reynolds's *The Sappho Companion* and especially Charles Gounod's *Sapho* (premiered by the Paris Opera, 1851).

On the new fragments first published in 2004 and 2014, see the technical article by Simon Burris, Jeffrey Fish, and Dirk Obbink, "New Fragments of Book 1 of Sappho" (*Zeitschrift für Papyrologie und Epigraphik*, 2014); and these more accessible works: Ellen Greene and Marilyn Skinner, *The New Sappho on Old Age: Textual and Philosophical Issues* (Harvard University Press, 2009), Dynamic Online Version: http://chs.harvard.edu/CHS/article/display/3534; and Dirk Obbink, "New Poems by Sappho" (*The Times Literary Supplement*, 5 February 2014: http://www.the-tls.co.uk/tls/public/article1371516.ece).

Other studies cited in the introduction are: Anne Carson, "The Justice of Aphrodite in Sappho 1" *Transactions of the American Philological Association* 110 (1980): 135–42 (published under the name Anne Giacomelli); Sarah Mace, "Amour, Encore! The Development of δηὖτε in Archaic Lyric," *Greek, Roman, and Byzantine Studies* 34 (1993): 335–364; and Ulrich von Wilamowitz-Moellendorff, *Sappho und Simonides, Untersuchungen über griechische Lyriker* (Weidmann, 1913).

Pamela Gordon
University of Kansas

3

to give

gloried
beautiful and noble
your friends, and you hurt me
blame

swollen
have enough   for the thought
mine not so
is disposed

I understand
of vileness

other
minds
blessed one

4

heart
completely
I can

may it be mine
to shine back
lovely face

stained

3. From a seventh-century C.E. parchment and a third-century C.E. Oxyrhynchus papyrus (P. Berol. 5006 and P. Oxy. 424).

4. From a seventh-century C.E. parchment (P. Berol. 5006).

Papyrus Sappho Obbink

You're always chattering about Charaxus
pulling in with a full cargo. I think Zeus
and the other gods know about that, but you
needn't dwell on it.

Just send me off to pray over and over
to Hera, imploring the queen of heaven
that my brother does sail his ship safely
into our home port

and finds me in one piece. Let's turn over
everything else to the divine powers.
Bright skies do sometimes appear suddenly
after great storms,

and if the lord of Olympus wills it,
a spirit from above will steer people clear
of all their troubles, blessing them
with happiness and wealth.

As for us, if Larichus would lift his head
and actually become a man some day,
all of our heavy-heartedness will then
instantly dissolve.

* Papyrus Sappho Obbink (not in Campbell). From a new Oxyrhynchus papyrus published by Dirk Obbink in 2014 (P. Sapph. Obbink).

8

Atthis, for you

9

summon to you
entirely
feast

in season fulfill
as long as I live

15

blessed one
lovely braids

absolved of all her previous sins

with good fortune harbor

O Cypris, may Dorikha find you
most bitter, may she not boast
how she came a second time
to her heart's desire.

8. From a second-century C.E. Oxyrhynchus papyrus (P. Oxy. 2289 fr. 3).

9. From a second-century C.E. Oxyrhynchus papyrus (P. Oxy. 2289 fr. 4).

15. From a second-century C.E. Oxyrhynchus papyrus (P. Oxy. 1231 frr. 1 and 3).

16i

Some say an army on horseback, some say on foot,
and some say ships are the most beautiful things
on this black earth, but I say
it is whatever you love.

It's easy to show this. Just look
at Helen, beautiful herself
beyond anything human, and she left
her perfect husband

and went sailing off to Troy
without a thought for her child
or her dear parents, led astray

lightly
reminding me of Anactoria
who is gone

and whose lovely walk
and bright, shimmering face
I would rather see than all the chariots
and armed men in Lydia.

16i. (Campbell 16, lines 1–20). From two second-century C.E. Oxyrhynchus papyri and a second- to third-century C.E. papyrus (P. Oxy. 1231 fr. 1, P. Oxy. 2166[a] 2, and *P.S.I.* 123).

16ii

but it cannot be
        humans pray   to share

and from the unexpected

17

May your graceful form glimmer
close to me as I pray, Lady Hera,
goddess beseeched by Atreus' sons,
glorious kings

who performed many heroic deeds
first at Troy and then on the sea
but could not complete their journey's end
here to this island
until they called upon you and on Zeus
and Thyone's lovely son Dionysus.
So also now be gracious to me
as to them of old

Holy and fair
maidens
around

to be
                to reach

16ii. (Campbell 16, lines 21–32, with gaps). From two second-century C.E. Oxyrhynchus papyri and a second- to third-century C.E. papyrus (P. Oxy. 1231 fr. 1, P. Oxy. 2166[a] 2, and *P.S.I.* 123).

17. From two second-century C.E. Oxyrhynchus papyri and a second- to third-century C.E. papyrus (P. Oxy. 1231 fr. 1, P. Oxy. 2166[a] 2, and *P.S.I.* 123).

18

all   to say   my tongue
to tell stories   and a man   greater

19

waiting   offerings
having fine   going   for we know
of works   later   and towards Cydro
says this

20

sheen, but also

with good luck . . . gain the harbor
of the black earth

sailors   huge gusts   on land

sail   cargo

flowing   many

tasks   dry land

18. From a second-century C.E. Oxyrhynchus papyrus (P. Oxy. 1231 fr. 1).

19. From a second-century C.E. Oxyrhynchus papyrus (P. Oxy. 1231 fr. 2).

20. From two second-century C.E. Oxyrhynchus papyri (P. Oxy. 1231 fr. 9 and P. Oxy. 2166[a]4[A]).

21

lament
  trembling

  the old man's skin already
wraps around
    takes wing pursuing

illustrious lady
  having taken
sing to us

violet-robed one

especially

she wanders

21. From a second-century C.E. Oxyrhynchus papyrus (P. Oxy. 1231 fr. 10).

22

hurt
work
face honored
unpleasant
but if not, winter
painless

Abanthis, take your lyre and sing
Of Gongyla, while Desire once again
flutters around
the beautiful girl. Her dress
excited you when you saw it,
and I am glad,
for the holy Cyprian herself
blamed me

when I prayed
this word
I want

22. From a second-century C.E. Oxyrhynchus papyrus (P. Oxy. 1231 frr. 12 and 15).

31

Look at him, just like a god,
that man sitting across from you,
whoever he is, listening to your
close sweet voice,

your irresistible laughter, and O yes
it sets my heart racing—
one glance at you and I can't
get any words out,

my voice cracks, a thin flame
runs under my skin,
my eyes see nothing,
my ears ring,

a cold sweat pours down my body,
I tremble all over, turn
paler than grass, and it seems that I'm
just a shade from dead.

But I must bear it, since a poor . . .

31. Longinus, a first-century C.E. critic who writes about the quality of thought and style (including the emotional element) that makes writing sublime, uses this poem in his work *On the Sublime* to illustrate excellence resulting from carefully chosen and combined details.

32

. . . who honored me by giving me their work

33

Gold-crowned Aphrodite, if only I
would share this fate

34

Stars around the beautiful moon
hide their brilliant forms
when at the full she lights the world

35

you either Cyprus or Paphos or Panormos

32. Apollonius Dyscolus, a second-century C.E. grammarian, uses this fragment in his book *On Pronouns* as an example of the Aeolic form *sphos*, "their."

33. Apollonius Dyscolus uses this fragment in his book *On Syntax* as an example of the word *aithe*, "if only."

34. Eustathius, a twelfth-century C.E. bishop and scholar, quotes these lines of Sappho in a discussion about the moon in his commentary on Homer's *Iliad* (8.555).

35. Strabo, a late first-century B.C.E. and early first-century C.E. historian and geographer, incorporates this line of Sappho into his *Geography*.

36

and I pine, and I yearn

37

may aching winds carry off
the one who reviles me

38

you singe us

39

sandals
of fine Lydian make, straps rainbow-dyed,
covered her feet

36. This phrase is recorded in the *Etymologicum Genuinum*, a ninth- to tenth-century C.E. work on the origins and meanings of words.

37. Both of these fragments appear in the *Etymologicum Genuinum*. The first is in a discussion of the Greek word *stalagmos*, "dripping." The second fragment illustrates a dialect consonant change to the Greek word *epiplesso*, "carry off."

38. Apollonius Dyscolus quotes this fragment in his *On Pronouns* to illustrate the Aeolic form of the Greek word for "us."

39. A scholiast (an ancient commentator who wrote notes in and around the main text) preserved this fragment in the margins of a manuscript of Aristophanes' play *Peace*. Aristophanes was a fifth-century B.C.E. Greek comedic playwright.

40

And to you I make an offering
of a white goat.

41

Towards you, lovely ones, my thoughts
never change.

42

their hearts have become cold
and they droop their wings

43

    disturbs   peace
    labor   mind
sits down
but come, my friends
    for day is near

40. Apollonius Dyscolus uses this line as an example of the Greek word *soi*, "to you," in his work *On Pronouns.*

41. Apollonius Dyscolus uses this line in his book *On Pronouns* to illustrate the Aeolic form of the word *ummin*, "to you."

42. A scholiast wrote this fragment in the margins of Pindar's tenth Pythian ode. Pindar was a fifth-century B.C.E. Greek lyric poet.

43. From a third-century C.E. Oxyrhynchus papyrus (P. Oxy. 1232 fr. 1).

44i

From Cyprus
a herald came
Idaeus   swift messenger

"From the rest of Asia   undying fame
Hector and his cohorts lead her, dancing-eyed,
from sacred Thebes and out of Plakos,
delicate Andromeda, in ships over the salt
sea, with many golden bracelets and clothing
shining purple, necklaces, jewels of many colors,
countless silver cups and ivory."
He spoke, and Hector's old father rose nimbly,
and the word spread throughout the broad city
to his dear ones. The Trojan women yoked mules
to their gliding chariots and went out in crowds
together with the slender-ankled girls,
Priam's daughters in a separate procession,
and the bachelors hitched up horses to their chariots,
young heroes in their might
        charioteers
                                        like gods
                                        holy throng
                                        to Ilion

    and there rose
flute's melody sweet with the lyre
the rattle of castanets, and shrill the maidens
sang the holy song and it reached bright heaven
eerie sound
and everywhere in the streets
mixing-bowls and cups
myrrh and cassia and frankincense blended,
and the older women with their alleluias
and all the men chanting the paeon
calling on Apollo, his lyre his bright bow,
praised Hector and Andromache, praised them as gods.

44i. (Campbell 44). From two third-century C.E. Oxyrhynchus papyri (P. Oxy. 1232 frr. 1 and 2 and P. Oxy. 2076).

44ii

. . . golden-haired Phoebus, whom the daughter of Coeus,
Leto, bore after lying with Zeus high in the clouds.
But Artemis swore an oath, the great oath of the gods:
"I swear by your head, I will be a virgin forever,
untamed, roaming the peaks of the lonely mountains,
hunting wild beasts. Come, nod assent for my sake."
So she spoke, and the father of the blessed gods nodded.
Gods and men alike call her the Virgin, Deer-slayer,
the Huntress, giving her these great titles. And Eros,
loosener of limbs, never comes near her . . .

the Muses' splendid
makes and the Graces'
to the slender
do not forget the anger
for mortals

45

as long as you are willing

44ii. (Campbell 44A). From a second- or third-century C.E. papyrus. Some editors speculate that this fragment may have been written by Alcaeus, a contemporary of Sappho (P. Fouad 239).

45. Apollonius Dyscolus uses this line in his book *On Pronouns* to illustrate the Aeolic form *ummes*, "you."

Papyrus Oxyrhynchus 1787

having fled
bitten

named you
put success in my mouth

58i

violet-robed Muses' gifts, girls,
the clear-toned, melodious lyre.

my skin once soft, but age now
my black hair has become

My heart is heavy, and my knees will not carry me,
though once they were light as a fawn's in the dance.

I lament this constantly, but what can be done?
There is no way for a human not to grow old.

They always said rose-armed Dawn loved Tithonus
and took him away, a beautiful young boy,

to the edge of the world. But in time grey old age
seized him, even though he slept with an immortal.

***Papyrus Oxyrhynchus 1787 (not in Campbell). From a third-century C.E. Oxyrhynchus papyrus discovered in the early twentieth century, which places this fragment before poem 58i (P. Oxy. 1787 fr. 1).

58i. (Campbell 58). From a third-century C.E. Oxyrhynchus papyrus and an early third-century B.C.E. papyrus published by Gronewald and Daniel in 2004. (P. Oxy. 1787 fr. 1 and P. Köl. inv. 21351 and 21376).

58ii

thinks
might send with

But I love delicacy   and this has won for me
radiant passion and the beauty of the sun.

59

loves

new

58ii. (Campbell 58). From a third-century C.E. Oxyrhynchus papyrus, which places this fragment after poem 58i. Fragment 58ii was long accepted as a continuation of poem 58i, until a new papyrus discovered in 2004 omitted it from the end of the poem (P. Oxy. 1787 frr. 1 and 2).

59. (not in Campbell). From a third-century C.E. Oxyrhynchus papyrus (P. Oxy. 1787 fr. 2).

60

happening upon
wish
fulfill my plan
I call
after my heart at once
all you want to get
fight at my side
obeying the voluptuous one
for you know well
in a year
broken

62

you shrank back
laurel when
everything sweeter
than that
and for the women
traveler
scarcely ever heard
soul beloved
to be such now
to come gentle
you got there first, beautiful
and the clothes

60. From a third-century C.E. Oxyrhynchus papyrus (P. Oxy. 1787 fr. 44).

62. From a third-century C.E. Oxyrhynchus papyrus (P. Oxy. 1787 fr. 3).

63

black dream
you come when sleep comes
sweet god, truly dreadful agony
to keep apart the power
but I have hope not to share
nothing of the blessed ones
for it would not be so
playthings
and may there be for me
for them everything

65

Sappho, I love you
on Cyprus queen
and yet great
all upon whom shining
everywhere fame
even in Acheron you

63. From a third-century C.E. Oxyrhynchus papyrus (P. Oxy. 1787 fr. 3).

65. From a third-century C.E. Oxyrhynchus papyrus (P. Oxy. 1787 fr. 4).

67

and this
destructive spirit
truly did not love
now because
the cause neither
nothing much

68

for me from the
yet became
her like the goddesses
sinful
Andromeda
blessed goddess
behavior
did not restrain insolence
sons of Tyndareus
graceful
ingenuous no longer
Megara

67. From a third-century C.E. Oxyrhynchus papyrus (P. Oxy. 1787 fr. 5).

68. From a third-century C.E. Oxyrhynchus papyrus (P. Oxy. 1787 fr. 7).

70

I will go

Harmonia
wonderful choir
trilling

71

Mica
but I will not allow you
you chose the friendship of Penthilus' house
you wicked thing
a sweet little song
softly voiced
trilling nightingales
dewy

73

Aphrodite
sweet-worded
might throw
having
sit
blossoms
lovely dew

70. From a third-century C.E. Oxyrhynchus papyrus (P. Oxy. 1787 fr. 13).

71. From a third-century C.E. Oxyrhynchus papyrus (P. Oxy. 1787 fr. 6).

73. From a third-century C.E. Oxyrhynchus papyrus (P. Oxy. 1787 fr. 11).

81

Wreathe your lovely hair with garlands, Dika,
weave stems of anise with your tender hands.
The Graces love to see you crowned with flowers,
but they will turn away from your unwreathed head.

82

Mnasidika is more shapely than tender Gyrinno

84

Artemis

85

so that the old man

81. Explaining why we should wear garlands, Athenaeus quotes these lines in *The Learned Banquet*. This quote is supplemented by a third-century C.E. Oxyrhynchus papyrus (P. Oxy. 1787 fr. 33).

82. Hephaestion quotes these lines in his *Handbook on Meter* as an example of acatalectic tetrameter.

84. From a third-century C.E. Oxyrhynchus papyrus (P. Oxy. 1787 frr. 37 and 41).

85. From a third-century C.E. Oxyrhynchus papyrus (P. Oxy. 1787 fr. 38).

86

aegis-bearing
Cytherea pray
having her heart
hear my prayer, if ever before
leaving
to my
difficult

88

you might wish
few
to be carried
sweeter to look at
and you yourself know
has forgotten
someone might say
for I will
love
as long as in me
will be a concern
I claim to have been a trustworthy friend
painful
bitter
but know this
I shall love

86. From a third-century C.E. Oxyrhynchus papyrus (P. Oxy. 1787 fr. = P. Oxy. 2166[d]1).

88. From a late second- or early third-century C.E. papyrus (P. Oxy. 2290).

91

having never found her more annoying
than you, Irana

92

robe
and
saffron
purple robe
cloaks
garlands
beautiful
Phrygian
purple

91. Hephaestion quotes this line in his *Handbook on Meter* as a second example of acatalectic tetrameter.

92. From a sixth-century C.E. parchment (P. Berol. 9722 fol. 1).

94

Truly I wish I were dead.
She was weeping when she left me,

and said many things to me, and said this:
"How much we have suffered, Sappho.
Truly, I do not want to leave you."

And I answered her:
"Farewell. Go, and remember me.
You know how we care for you.

And if you should not, I want
to remind you
                    our moments of grace

the many garlands of violets,
roses and crocuses
                    you put on my head,

and the many necklaces
woven of flowers
                    on my soft skin
all   the myrrh
expensive
you anointed   royal

and on soft coverlets
tender
quenched your desire

neither any   nor
shrine
from which we held back

nor grove   dance
                    noise

94. From a sixth-century C.E. parchment, supplemented by Lobel (P. Berol. 9722 fol. 2 and Lobel Σ.μ. p.79).

95

Gongyla . . .

surely some sign . . .
for all, especially . . .
Hermes came in . . .

I said, "O Lord . . .
for by the blessed goddess, I
do not enjoy being above ground

but am gripped by a desire to die
and to see the lotus-covered,
dewy banks of the Acheron . . .

95. From a sixth-century C.E. parchment (P. Berol. 9722 fol. 4).

96

from Sardis
often turning your mind here

we thought you were like a goddess
everyone looked at you
she loved the way you moved in the dance

now among the women in Lydia

as at sunset the rose-fingered moon
outshines all stars, spreading her light
over the salt sea, the flowering fields,

and the glimmering dew falls, roses
bloom amid delicate starflowers
chervil and sweet clover

she walks back and forth, remembering
her beloved Atthis,
the tender soul consumed with grief

to go there   this
mind   much
talks   in the middle

It is not easy for us to equal
goddesses in beauty

Aphrodite
poured nectar from
a golden

with her hands   Persuasion

the Geraesteum
dear ones

nothing

96. From a sixth-century C.E. parchment, supplemented by Lobel (P. Berol. 9722 fol. 5 and Lobel Σ.μ. p.80).

98

for my mother once told me

that in her youth it was considered elegant
for a girl to put her hair up
in a purple headband—indeed it was—

but for the girl with hair more golden-red
than a flaming torch it was better
to do it up in wreaths of blooming flowers.

Recently an embroidered headband
from Sardis
Ionian cities

But, Kleis, I don't know where to get
an embroidered headband for you.
the Mytilenean, though

to get

embroidery

reminders of
exile of Cleanax's sons

dreadful loss

98. The first lines (ending at "Ionian cities") come from a third-century B.C.E. papyrus, one of the oldest extant papyri of Sappho, now in Copenhagen. The remainder of the poem is from another papyrus fragment housed in Milan (P. Haun. 301 and P. Medio. ed. Vogliano).

99

after a little
Polyanax's sons
plucking strings
women using plectrums
kindly
quivers

Son of Leto and Zeus
come to your rites
leaving wooded Gryneia
oracle
hymn sister

Polyanax's sons
I want to point out the mad one

100

And covered her well with soft, woolen cloth

99. From a third-century C.E. papyrus. Some editors speculate that this fragment may have been written by Alcaeus (P. Oxy. 2291).

100. Pollux quotes this fragment in his *Vocabulary*.

101

and handkerchiefs . . . purple, scented
from Phocaea
expensive gifts

102

Sweet mother, I can no longer work the loom.
Slender Aphrodite has made me fall in love with a boy.

103i

for to speak
the bride with beautiful feet
Zeus' violet-robed daughter
putting aside anger violet-robed
holy graces and Pierian Muses
whenever songs . . . the mind
she hearing a clear song
bridegroom, for irksome companions
for her hair, setting down the lyre
gold-sandaled Dawn

101. Athenaeus quotes these lines in a reference to handkerchiefs in *The Learned Banquet.*

102. Hephaestion quotes these lines in his *Handbook on Meter* as an example of an antispastic meter.

103i. (Campbell 103). From a second-century C.E. papyrus, part of an ancient commentary that lists the first lines or partial first lines of ten different poems by Sappho (P. Oxy. 2294).

103ii

bedroom
  bride with lovely feet

104i

Hesperos,
you bring all that the bright dawn scattered—
the lamb, the kid, the child to its mother.

104ii

of all stars the most beautiful

103ii. (Campbell 103B). From a late second- or early third-century C.E. papyrus (P. Oxy. 2308).

104i. (Campbell 104). This fragment is quoted in a work entitled *On Style*, a book of literary criticism. Although *On Style* is traditionally attributed to Demetrius of Phalerum (born c. 350 B.C.E.), the authorship is not certain.

104ii. (Campbell 104). This fragment is quoted by Himerius, a fourth-century C.E. rhetorician, in his *Orations*.

117i

Farewell to the bride, and farewell to the bridegroom.

117ii

polished doorway

118

Come, divine lyre-shell, tell me,
become a speaking voice.

119

dripping, half-worn cloth

117i. (Campbell 117). Hephaestion quotes this line in his *Handbook on Meters* as an example of catalectic meter.

117ii. (Campbell 117A). Hesychius of Alexandria, a fourth-century C.E. Greek grammarian, quotes this phrase in his *Lexicon*.

118. Hermogenes quotes this fragment in *Kinds of Style* as an example of the "sweet" effect of personification.

119. A scholiast uses this phrase to clarify an unusual reference to a napkin in Aristophanes' comedy *Plutus*.

120

I am not of those backbiters.
I have a kind heart.

121

But if you are my friend,
go to a younger woman's bed;
for I will not endure an affair
in which I am older than the man.

122

a child, very soft, picking flowers

123

Golden-sandaled Dawn had just . . .

120. The unknown compiler of the *Etymologicum Magnum*, a lexicon published in Constantinople circa 1150 C.E., quotes this fragment as an example of the word *abakēs*, "gentle."

121. Stobaeus, in his *Anthology*, quotes these lines in a discussion of age differences in love.

122. Athenaeus, in *The Learned Banquet*, includes this line of Sappho in a discussion of flower gathering; Sappho apparently says that she saw this child.

123. Ammonius, a third-century C.E. Greek philosopher, quotes this fragment in *On Similar but Different Words*, claiming that Sappho's use of the adverb *artios*, "just now," is incorrect.

124

and you yourself, Calliope,

125

I myself once wove garlands

126

Sleeping on the breast of your tender companion

127

Come here again, Muses, leaving the golden . . .

124. In his *Handbook on Meter*, Hephaestion refers to this fragment for its spondaic line-beginning.

125. A scholiast on Aristophanes quotes this line in order to use Sappho's mention of garlands as a precedent for a mention of garlands in Aristophanes' comedy *Thesmophoriazousae*.

126. This fragment is quoted in the *Etymologicum Genuinum* in reference to an unusual word for "sleep."

127. Hephaestion quotes this fragment in his *Handbook on Meter* as an example of ithyphallic meter.

128

Come here now, tender Graces and lovely-haired Muses

129i

You have forgotten me

129ii

Or you love someone else more

130

Eros once more, limbslackener, makes me shudder,
sweetbitter, irresistible, creeping thing

128. In his *Handbook on Meter*, Hephaestion uses this line to demonstrate choriambic tetrameter.

129i. (Campbell 129). Apollonius Dyscolus quotes this line in his work *On Pronouns* to illustrate a form of the Greek word for "me."

129ii. (Campbell 129). Apollonius Dyscolus quotes this line directly after fragment 129i in his work *On Pronouns*; it is unclear whether they are part of the same poem.

130. In his *Handbook on Meter*, Hephaestion uses these lines to illustrate one variety of dactylic tetrameter.

131

Atthis, you've grown to hate the very thought of me,
and you fly off to Andromeda.

132

I have a beautiful child who looks like
golden flowers, my beloved Kleis,
whom I would not trade for all Lydia
or for lovely . . .

133i

Andromeda has fine compensation . . .

131. Hephaestion quotes these lines in his *Handbook on Meter* as examples of tetrameter verse.

132. Hephaestion includes this fragment in his book *Handbook on Meter* to explain aspects of trochaic meter.

133i. (Campbell 133). Hephaestion quotes this fragment in his *Handbook on Meters* as an example of anaclastic meter.

133ii

"Sappho, why . . . blessed Aphrodite . . .

134

I really talked with you in a dream,
Cyprogeneia . . .

135

O Irana, why does the swallow,
Pandion's daughter, . . . me?

136

Spring's messenger, the nightingale's
pining voice . . .

133ii. (Campbell 133). Hephaestion quotes this fragment along with fragment 133i in his *Handbook on Meters* as another example of anaclastic meter.

134. Hephaestion quotes this fragment in his *Handbook on Meter* to illustrate acatalectic meter.

135. In his *Handbook on Meter*, Hephaestion uses this line to exemplify an Ionic meter.

136. A scholiast commenting on the play *Electra* (by the fifth-century B.C.E. Greek tragedian Sophocles) remarks on a similarity of expression concerning the nightingale by quoting this line of Sappho.

137

"I want to say something, but shame prevents me."

"But if your desire were for the noble and good
and if your tongue were not brewing up evil,
shame would not turn your eyes glassy.
You would speak out for what is right."

138

Stand before me as a friend.
Spread out the grace that is in your eyes.

139

the gods . . . immediately without tears

137. Aristotle, a fourth-century B.C.E. philosopher, quotes these lines in a discussion on shame in his *Rhetoric.* He attributes (probably wrongly) the first two lines to the poet Alcaeus.

138. In *The Learned Banquet*, Athenaeus quotes this fragment, suggesting that Sappho would use these lines to mock a vain man.

139. From a third-century C.E. Oxyrhynchus papyrus of a text of Philo, a late first- and early second-century grammarian who quotes Sappho's advice about the gods. The text is supplemented by Lobel (P. Oxy. 1356 fol.4a and Lobel Σ.μ. p.55).

140

"Delicate Adonis is dying, Cytherea. What shall we do?"

"Beat your breasts, maidens, and rend your tunics."

141

A bowl of nectar had been mixed there.
Hermes took the pitcher and poured for the gods,
who all tipped their cups,
wishing the bridegroom all their very best.

142

Leto and Niobe were very dear friends.

143

Golden chickpeas grew on the banks

140. Hephaestion, a second-century C.E. grammarian, quotes this selection in his *Handbook on Meter* to illustrate a catalectic line.

141. In *The Learned Banquet*, Athenaeus uses this selection in a discussion of Hermes.

142. In *The Learned Banquet*, Athenaeus quotes this line in a discussion of the use of the word *hetaera*, "companion."

143. Athenaeus quotes this line in a section on chick-peas in *The Learned Banquet.*

144

they were disgusted
with Gorgo

145

Don't move piles of gravel

146

For me neither honey nor the honey bee

147

Someone, I say, will remember us

144. Herodian quotes this fragment in *On the Declension of Nouns* to illustrate the different forms of nouns that end in "o."

145. A scholiast on Apollonius' *Argonautica*, a third-century B.C.E. epic poem that tells the story of Jason and the Golden Fleece, refers to this fragment for its use of the word *cherados*, "pile of pebbles."

146. Tryphon, a first-century B.C.E. grammarian, quotes this in his work *Figures of Speech* as an example of a proverb.

147. Dio Chrysostom, a first-century C.E. Roman historian, philosopher, and orator, quotes this line in his *Discourses.*

148

Wealth without riches is no harmless neighbor.
Blending both holds the height of happiness.

149

When night-long sleep seizes them

150

For lamentation is not right in the house of those
who attend the Muses. It would not be fitting for us.

151

the black sword of night in my eyes

148. A scholiast on Pindar's second Olympian Ode uses these lines to explain why Pindar thinks wealth and virtue should go hand in hand.

149. Apollonius Dyscolus quotes this fragment in his *Pronouns* as an example of the pronoun *sphi*, "to them."

150. Maximus of Tyre quotes this selection in his *Orations* as an example of anger at those who are mourning.

151. From the *Etymologicum Genuinum* in reference to a rare word for "sleep." The translation follows a variant reading that suggests the word "sword."

160

I will sing these beautifully now
to my companions' delight

161

you guarded her
                                        the bridegrooms
                              cities' kings

162

with what eyes

163

the one I care for

160. Athenaeus quotes this line in his *The Learned Banquet.*

161. From a papyrus discovered by Urbain Bouriant in Egypt in the late nineteenth century (P. Bouriant. 8.91ss).

162. Georgios Choeroboskos, an early ninth-century C.E. grammarian, uses this fragment as an example of an alternate form of the word for "what."

163. Julian the Apostate quotes this phrase in addressing the recipient of a letter.

164

she calls her child

165

that man seems to himself

166

They say that Leda once found
a hyacinth-blue egg, covered . . .

167

far whiter than an egg

164. Apollonius Dyscolus quotes this phrase in his *On Pronouns* as an example of an unusual Aeolic spelling.

165. Apollonius Dyscolus quotes this phrase in his *On Pronouns* as another example of the same unusual spelling.

166. Athenaeus quotes these lines in *The Learned Banquet*, on Sappho's trisyllabic use of the word *oion*, "egg."

167. In *The Learned Banquet*, Athenaeus quotes this phrase as another example of Sappho's use of the word for "egg."

168i

The moon has set,
and the Pleiades.
Midnight.
            The hour has gone by.
I sleep alone.

168ii

embroidered Earth, encircled with flowers

169i

I might lead

169ii

wedding presents

168i. (Campbell 168B). Hephaestion includes this fragment of Sappho in his *Handbook on Meter* to demonstrate a type of Ionic tetrameter.

168ii. (Campbell 168C). This fragment is quoted by the author of *On Style* (see note on fragment 114) to demonstrate how attractive words produce a charming effect.

169i. (Campbell 169). A scholiast on Homer's *Iliad* refers to this verb form to compare Sappho's use of the verb to Homer's.

169ii. (Campbell 169A). Hesychius includes this fragment in his *Lexicon*.

170

Aega

171

harmless

172

a gift of pain

173

climbing vine

170. In his *Geography*, Strabo quotes Sappho's use of the name of the promontory Aega.

171. Photius, a ninth-century C.E. scholar and ruler of Constantinople, includes Sappho's use of this word in his *Lexicon*.

172. Maximus of Tyre quotes this as an epithet of Eros in his *Orations*.

173. Choeroboskos quotes Sappho's use of this word in a discussion of feminine noun forms.

174

channel

175

dawn

176

bass lyre

177

short dress

174. Orion of Thebes, a fifth-century C.E. grammarian, includes Sappho's use of this word in his *Lexicon*.

175. Apollonius Dyscolus includes Sappho's use of this word in his *On Adverbs*.

176. In his *The Learned Banquet*, Athenaeus says that Sappho mentions this instrument.

177. Pollux includes Sappho's use of this term in his *Vocabulary*.

178

Gello

179

cosmetic bag

180

Holder (Zeus)

181

crossable

178. Zenobius, a second-century C.E. rhetorician, quotes this fragment in his *Proverbs*.

179. Phrynichus, a second-century C.E. rhetorician, quotes Sappho's use of this term in a discussion on cosmetic bags in his *Sophistic Preparation*.

180. Hesychius quotes Sappho's use of this word in his *Lexicon*.

181. A scholiast on Dionysius of Thrace, a second- and early first-century B.C.E. grammarian, quotes Sappho's use of this form as an addition to the information Dionysius provides.

182

I might go

183

down-rushing

184

danger

185

honey-voiced

soft-voiced

182. A scholiast on Homer's *Iliad* quotes Sappho's use of this word (see note 169i).

183. Porphyry, a third-century C.E. philosopher, quotes Sappho's use of this phrase in his *Homeric Questions.*

184. Choeroboskos quotes Sappho's use of this word in his *On the Canons of Theodosius.*

185. Philostratus, a late second- and early third-century C.E. sophist, quotes the first of these epithets in his *Imagines.* Aristaenetus, a fifth- or sixth-century letter-writer, quotes the second in his *Love Letters.*

186

Medea

187

the Muses'

188

word-weaver

189

soda

186. John of Alexandria, a sixth-century C.E. grammarian and theologian, quotes Sappho's use of this name in his *Rules of Accentuation*.

187. The author of the *Homeric Parsings* quotes this plural possessive form (see note 109).

188. In his *Orations*, Maximus of Tyre quotes this phrase, which he says Sappho uses to refer to Eros.

189. Phrynichus quotes Sappho's use of this word in his *Attic Words and Phrases*.

3

On Pelagon the fisherman's tomb his father Meniscus placed
his creel and oar, memorials of a wretched life.

Epitaphs for Sappho

4

Sappho lies beneath you, Aeolian earth, sung
by the immortal Muses as the mortal Muse
whom Cypris and Eros together reared, and with whom
Persuasion wove the Pierians' ever-living wreath,
Hellas' joy and your island's glory. You Fates
who twirl the triple thread on your spindle,
why did you not spin undying day for the singer
who turned her mind to the Muses' deathless gifts?

3. (Campbell 159D). This epigram survives in the *Palatine Anthology* (7.505). It is attributed to Sappho.

4. (Campbell *Testimonia* 27). This epigram survives in the *Palatine Anthology* (7.14). It is attributed to Antipater of Sidon, a late second-century B.C.E. Greek poet.

5

When you pass by this Aeolian tomb do not say
that I, the poet from Mitylene, am dead.
Men's hands built this, and such human works
will vanish into swift oblivion.
But if you measure me by the divine Muses, a flower
from each of whom I set beside my nine books,
you will know I escaped Hades' gloom, and that the name
of Sappho the lyric poet will rise with every sun.

Tributes to Sappho

6

Sweetest support for young lovers' passions,
Sappho: Pieria and ivied Helicon
honor you alongside the Muses, whose very breath
you breathe, Muse from Aeolian Eresus.
Or Hymen, the wedding god, holding his torch
hovers with you over bridal beds.
Or, lamenting with Aphrodite as she mourns Adonis,
you look upon the sacred grove of the Blest.
Wherever you are, Lady, greetings as to a goddess,
for we still have your immortal daughters, your songs.

5. (Campbell *Testimonia* 28). This epigram survives in the *Palatine Anthology* (7.17). It is attributed to Tullius Laurea, a freedman of Cicero who wrote in the first-century B.C.E.

6. (Campbell *Testimonia* 58). This epigram survives in the *Palatine Anthology* (7.407). It is attributed to Dioscorides, a Greek epigrammatist of the third-century B.C.E.

7

. . . weaving in many flowers, lilies of Anyte and Moera,
a few of Sappho's, but these are all roses . . .

8

My name is Sappho, and I surpassed all women poets
by as much as Homer surpassed the men.

9

Some say there are only nine Muses. How shortsighted!
Look and you'll see: Sappho of Lesbos makes ten.

7. (Campbell *Testimonia* 43). This selection was written by Meleager of Gadara for his *The Garland*, a first-century B.C.E. collection of poems and epigrams. This fragment of *The Garland* survives in the *Palatine Anthology* (4.1.5s).

8. (Campbell *Testimonia* 57). This epigram survives in the *Palatine Anthology* (7.15). It is attributed to Antipater of Sidon.

9. (Campbell *Testimonia* 60). This epigram survives in the *Palatine Anthology* (9.506). It is attributed to Plato, a late fifth- and early fourth-century B.C.E. Greek philosopher.

Heroides 15, Ovid's Unanswered Letter from Sappho to Phaon

When the acclaimed American dancer Isadora Duncan visited Greece, she neglected Lesbos. But in a 1903 trip to the island of Lefkada on the opposite side of the Greek world, she visited the Leucadian cliffs from which Sappho (according to a fictional tradition) jumped to her death for unrequited love. The story about Sappho's suicide is based not on historical fact but on a Greek legend that she was spurned by a young man named Phaon. According to "On Incredible Events," an obscure source on Greek mythology attributed to an equally obscure "Pseudo-Palaephatus," Phaon was an honorable old ferryman on Lesbos who was transformed into a beautiful youth by Aphrodite. Other sources add that Aphrodite—who had a penchant for mortal men—fell in love with Phaon and hid him among the lettuces (as she did with Adonis, another young favorite). Phaon's presence in Sappho's biography may be due to a misinterpretation of a poem by Sappho in which Aphrodite (rather than Sappho) lamented the loss of Phaon, or perhaps there were poems about Phaon in which Sappho merged her own voice with Aphrodite's.

The most memorable of the surviving sources for the tale of Sappho and Phaon is the following poem by the first-century B.C.E. Roman poet Ovid. The work belongs to the *Heroides*, a collection of fifteen letters (in Latin verse) from the great abandoned heroines of Greek and Roman mythology, including Ariadne, Dido, Medea, and Phaedra. Sappho's presence among these traditional characters demonstrates her status as a mythic figure, and perhaps we should view Ovid's treatment of Sappho's erotic history within this mythological context. As mentioned in this edition's introduction to the poems of Sappho, Ovid's "Sappho" describes her attachment to Phaon as a monumental departure from her love for Anactoria, Atthis, and the rest of "that Lesbian crowd." But this Sappho's conversion from lover of women to a woman who loves a man also betrays a Roman context. We do not have Greek documents from the next few centuries after Sappho that unambiguously assign to her (or to other women) a particular sexual orientation, but some Roman texts express disgust and contempt for a type of supposedly monstrous woman called a *tribas* (plural: *tribades*). *Tribades* allegedly haunt graveyards and run wild at night, and the height of their monstrousness is that they have sex with other women. For a *tribas* to love a man would indeed require a radical transformation.

If you were so fixed on leaving me,
  you could have at least left with more grace.
All you had to say was, "Goodbye, Lesbian girl."
  No tears, no kisses, no premonition of loss.
I have nothing of you except the wrong you did me,
  and you have no token of your lover.
I gave you no parting words, nor would I have given you any
  except perhaps that you not forget me.
I swear to you by our love (may it never disappear!)
  and by the nine Muses who are my gods,
when someone (I don't remember who) told me, "He's left
    you,"
  for a long time I could not cry or speak.
My eyes wouldn't form tears, words wouldn't form in my
    mouth,
  and my chest was a knot of frozen pain.
Then my grief found itself, and I wasn't ashamed
  to beat my breast, tear my hair out and wail,
as if I were a mother carrying the corpse
  of her beloved son to the funeral pyre.
Charaxus, my brother, just loved it, got fat
  on my sorrow, paraded before me,
saying out loud, to make my grief seem shameful:
  "Why is she so sad? Is her daughter dead?"
Modesty and love don't come to the same thing.
  The whole world saw my torn naked breast.

You're all I care about, Phaon. My dreams bring you back,
  dreams brighter than beautiful daylight.
I find you there though you are gone from these parts.
  But sleep can't bring joy that lasts long enough.
In my fantasies I press my neck
  into your arms, or yours into mine,
feel the deep tongue kisses you used to give
  and receive, the soft caresses, the words—
I actually speak the words—it all seems so real,
  my lips are real, all my senses alert.
I'm embarrassed to say more, but it all happens,
  and it feels so good, and I can't stay dry.

Then the sun reveals itself and everything else,
   and I complain that sleep has left me so soon.
I head for the woods, the caves, as if these could help,
   woods and caves that know my secret pleasures.
And there I run like a woman possessed,
   hair fanning out along my neck.
The caves are scaly with volcanic rock: they seem
   to my eyes like Mygdonian marble.
I find the forest that used to bed us down,
   the dark forest whose leaves covered us,
but I do not find my lord of the forest.
   The place is cheap ground: he gives it its worth.
But I recognized where the grass was pressed down,
   the familiar sod hollowed by our weight,
and I nestled in the spot where you once lay.
   The grass, still gracious, sopped up my tears.
The bare ruined branches seem also to lament,
   and the sweet birds sing no more their complaint.
Only the nightingale sings of her murdered son,
   the son she killed to punish her husband.
The nightingale sings of Itys, Sappho of lost love.
   The rest is silence, the silence of midnight.

There is a bright, sacred spring clearer than crystal—
   many think a spirit possesses the water—
and above it a lotus spreads its branches,
   a single tree grown to a grove,
and the earth is green with tender turf.
   Exhausted from weeping, I lay there to rest
when a Naiad appeared before my eyes,
   stood there and said: "Unrequited love?
You must go to Ambracia. Apollo on high
   looks down from the headlands on the sea that is known
as Actian and Leucadian. Deucalion, smoldering
   with love for Pyrrha, threw himself off there,
and hit the water with body unharmed. Submerged,
   the passion drained from his chest,
and Deucalion was relieved of his igneous love.
   It is a reliable local phenomenon.
Hurry up, then, to the Leucadian cliff,
   and don't be afraid to dive from the rock."

Voice and image faded together. I rose, terrified,
my eyes and cheeks still flooded with tears.
I'll go. Nymph, I'll find that rock, fear subdued
and banished by maddening passion.
Anything will be better than this. Breeze, support me,
bear my body lightly, and you, soft Eros,
feather me as I fall, lest I die and become
a blot to the honor of the Leucadian Sea.
Then I'll dedicate to Apollo our common lyre
and under it there will be a line or two:

"Sappho the poet to Apollo, *ex votis*:
the lyre that is my trademark and yours."

But why do you send me to the shores of Actium
when you could yourself retrace your steps?
You would be better for me than the Leucadian surf,
be my Apollo in kindness and looks.
Or could you bear, if I die, to be labeled my murderer,
crueler than any rock or sea?
How much better for my breast to be
pressed against yours than plunged upon rocks!
The very breast, Phaon, that you used to praise,
that seemed so often to breathe with genius.
I wish I were eloquent now. Grief stops my art,
all my genius is immobile with misery.
My old poetic power won't answer the call,
my plectrum and lyre lie mute with sorrow.

Lesbian islanders, married, engaged,
Lesbians catalogued on my Aeolian lyre,
Lesbians loved to my disgrace:
crowd around to hear my zither no more.
Phaon ("my Phaon" I almost said)
has stolen away all that you loved.
Bring him back and you'll have your poet back too:
he gives me my power and takes it away.

Do I accomplish anything with my prayers?
    Is his country heart moved or stiff with cold,
and do the winds bear off my words as they fall?
    The winds that bear off my words,
I wish they bore back your sails. If you had any feeling
    you wouldn't take so long to do what is right.

If you are coming back, preparing now
    to consecrate your stern,
why tear my heart with delay? Untie the hawser!
    Seaborn Venus protects lovers at sea,
The wind will keep you on course.
    Just untie the hawser!
Cupid himself will pilot your ship, sitting on the stern,
    his tender hand will spread and furl sail.

But if it is pleasant to have flown far from Pelasgian Sappho
    even though I don't deserve to be shunned,
at least let a cruel letter inform me of this,
    so I can seek my end in Leucadian waters.

Glossary

Abanthis A girl or woman mentioned by Sappho; nothing else is known about her. Sappho 22.

Acheron The "river of sorrow," one of the five rivers of the Underworld in Greek mythology; also a metonym for the Underworld as a whole. Sappho 65 and 95.

Actium (*Aktion* in Greek) Promontory in western Greece; location of a temple of Apollo. *Heroides* 15.

Adonis One of Aphrodite's mortal lovers. In many Greek traditions, his death while still a youth was the subject of great lamentation, particularly by women. Sappho 140; Epigram 6.

Aega Promontory on the coast of Asia Minor opposite Mytilene. Sappho 170.

Aegean Sea Part of the Mediterranean Sea, situated between mainland Greece and Asia Minor.

Aeolic Greek A set of dialects of ancient Greek spoken in Boeotia in central Greece, in Thessaly, on Lesbos, and in Greek colonies on the western coast of Asia Minor. Areas in which Aeolic was the primary dialect of Greek are sometimes described as Aeolian. Epigrams 4, 5, and 6.

Aethiopia Epithet of the Greek goddess Artemis, emphasizing her connections with the Upper Nile region and lands south of the Sahara Desert. Epigram 1.

Aetna Modern-day Mount Etna, a volcanic mountain on the east coast of Sicily. *Heroides* 15.

Alcaeus Contemporary of Sappho from MYTILENE. Alcaeus wrote lyric poetry and is said to have traded poems with Sappho. Several fragments unearthed in modern times are tentatively attributed to either Sappho or Alcaeus, since the two poets wrote in similar meters and styles. *Heroides* 15.

Alcman Seventh-century B.C.E. Greek lyric poet from SPARTA. He is known for his choral poetry, as well as his use of Asian and Lydian imagery.

Alexandria Capital and cultural center of HELLENISTIC Egypt, known for its great library dedicated to the MUSES, which burned sometime between the first-century B.C.E. and the fourth-century C.E.

Ambracia Ancient city on the western coast of the Greek mainland. *Heroides* 15.

Anacreon Sixth- and early fifth-century B.C.E. Greek lyric poet who lived and worked in Thrace, on the island of Samos, and in ATHENS. He was known for his odes and drinking songs.

Anactoria A girl or woman mentioned by Sappho; nothing else is known about her. Sappho 16i; *Heroides* 15.

Andromache Wife of HECTOR in Greek mythology. Sappho 44i.

Andromeda (1) A woman mentioned by Sappho. Some scholars posit that she was a rival poet, others that she was Sappho's rival in love. Sappho 68, 131, and 133i.

Andromeda (2) In Greek mythology, an Aethiopian princess chained to a rock and rescued by PERSEUS. Sappho 44i, *Heroides* 15.

Andros An island south of LESBOS in the AEGEAN SEA. Its name also means "man."

Anyte Early third-century B.C.E. Greek poet, known for her epigrams and epitaphs. She is one of the few female poets from the ancient Greek and Roman world whose work survives. Epigram 7.

Aphrodite Greek goddess of erotic love, sometimes identified as the mother of EROS. Sappho 1, 33, 73, 96, 102, 112, and 133ii; Epigram 6.

Apollo Greek god associated with the lyre and the MUSES; son of ZEUS and LETO. Sappho 44i, *Heroides* 15.

Archeanassa A girl or woman mentioned by Sappho; nothing else is known about her. Sappho 213i and 214i.

Archilochus Seventh-century B.C.E. Greek poet, known for his "abuse poetry," which revolved around insults and blame.

Ares Greek god of brutal warfare. Sappho 111.

Ariadne In Greek mythology, a princess of CRETE who became the wife of DIONYSUS. *Heroides* 15.

Arista A woman mentioned in an epigram attributed to Sappho; nothing else is known about her. Epigram 1.

Artemis Greek goddess of wild animals, chastity, and the hunt; daughter of ZEUS and LETO. Sappho 44ii and 84.

Asia Greek name for ASIA MINOR. Sappho 44i.

Asia Minor Peninsula, which makes up most of modern Turkey, location of the city of TROY.

Athens One of the largest and most prosperous city-states in ancient GREECE.

Atreus In Greek mythology, king of Mycenae in GREECE; father of Agamemnon and Menelaus, the brothers who started the Trojan War. Sappho 17.

Atthis A girl or woman, possibly a lover, mentioned by Sappho; nothing else is known about her. Sappho 8, 49i, 96, 131, and 214iii; *Heroides* 15.

Aurora Roman name for the Greek goddess DAWN. *Heroides* 15.

Bacchus Roman name for the Greek god Dionysus. *Heroides* 15.

Byzantine Period Period of Mediterranean history lasting from the fourth-century to the fifteenth-century C.E.

Calliope Muse of epic poetry. Sappho 124.

Cephalus In Greek mythology, a mortal lover of the goddess Dawn, who pined away for his wife until Dawn finally returned him to her. *Heroides* 15.

Charaxus According to ancient bibliographical sources, the eldest of Sappho's brothers, followed by Eurygius and Larichus. "Papyrus Sappho Obbink" and Sappho 213ii; *Heroides* 15.

Cleanax A man mentioned by Sappho. Cleanax may be another name for the tyrant Myrsilus, who was in power in Mytilene during Sappho's exile; or Myrsilus may be his son. Sappho 98.

Coeus In Greek mythology, a Titan, son of the earth and sky; the father of Leto. Sappho 44ii.

Constantinople Capital of the Byzantine Empire; modern Istanbul.

Crete A large Greek island south of mainland Greece in the Mediterranean Sea; the mythological home of Ariadne. Sappho 2.

Cupid Roman name for the Greek god Eros. *Heroides* 15.

Cydro A girl or woman mentioned by Sappho; nothing else is known about her. Sappho 19; *Heroides* 15.

Cyprian Epithet of the goddess Aphrodite that celebrates her birth on the Greek island Cyprus. Sappho 22.

Cypris Epithet of the goddess Aphrodite that celebrates her birth on the Greek island Cyprus. Sappho 2, 5, 15, and 26; Epigram 4.

Cyprogeneia Epithet of the goddess Aphrodite that celebrates her birth on the Greek island Cyprus. Sappho 134.

Cyprus A Greek island south of ASIA MINOR in the Mediterranean Sea, one of two possible birthplaces of the goddess APHRODITE. Sappho 35, 44i, and 65.

Cythera A Greek island south of mainland GREECE in the Mediterranean Sea, one of two possible birthplaces of the goddess APHRODITE.

Cytherea Epithet of the goddess APHRODITE that celebrates her birth on the Greek island CYTHERA. Sappho 86 and 140.

Daphne In Greek mythology, a NYMPH who swore an oath of eternal virginity. The god APOLLO fell in love with her and attempted to capture her, but she chose to become a tree instead. *Heroides* 15.

Dawn (*Eos* in Greek) Greek goddess known for her beauty and her love for mortal men, including TITHONUS. Sappho 6, 58i, 103i, 123, and 157.

Desire See EROS. Sappho 22.

Deucalion Husband of PYRRHA. When ZEUS destroyed most of the human race in a great flood Pyrrha and Deucalion survived by building an ark. *Heroides* 15.

Dido Mythological queen of Carthage in North Africa, who killed herself when the hero Aeneas left her. OVID wrote one of his *HEROIDES* from her point of view.

Dionysus Greek god of wine, mania, and theater, son of THYONE and ZEUS. Dionysus was known for his connections to the East and for his almost-feminine beauty. Sappho 17.

Dika A girl or woman mentioned by Sappho. Her name means "Justice." Sappho 81.

Dorian Greek A set of dialects of ancient Greek spoken in northwest and southern GREECE, Crete, and Greek colonies in southwestern ASIA MINOR.

Dorikha A woman mentioned by Sappho, possibly a lover of Sappho's brother CHARAXUS. Sappho 7 and 15.

Eresus Ancient town on Lesbos; the birthplace of Sappho. Epigram 6.

Eros Divine personification of Desire in Greek mythology. Eros is sometimes said to be a primordial force, but other sources identify him as the son of Aphrodite and Ares. Sappho 44ii, 47, 130, and 159; Epigram 4; *Heroides* 15.

Erycina Epithet of the Roman goddess Venus associated with a particular cult, which had a reputation for drawing the attention of prostitutes. *Heroides* 15.

Euphrates A river that defines the northeastern boundary of Asia Minor.

Eurygius According to ancient bibliographical sources, one of Sappho's brothers, along with Charaxus and Larichus.

Fates Trio of Greek goddesses who assigned the destinies of mortals. Epigram 4.

Gello A girl or woman mentioned by Sappho; nothing else is known about her. Sappho 178.

Geraesteum This may refer to a temple of the Greek sea god Poseidon at Geraestus on the Greek mainland. Sappho 96.

Gongyla A girl mentioned by Sappho; nothing else is known about her. Sappho 22, 95, and 213ii.

Gorgo A girl or woman mentioned by Sappho; nothing else is known about her. Sappho 29, 144, and 213i.

Graces Three Greek goddesses of grace and charm. Sappho 44ii, 53, 81, 103i, and 128.

Greece In ancient times, Greece was not one unified country, but a group of independent city-states and territories which were linked by their common language.

Gryneia Ancient Aeolic city on the western coast of Asia Minor, home to a cult of the god Apollo. Sappho 99.

Gyrinno A girl or woman mentioned by Sappho; nothing else is known about her. Sappho 29 and 82.

Hades Greek god who ruled the Underworld, or land of the dead; also a metonym for the Underworld as a whole. Sappho 55; Epigram 5.

Harmonia Minor Greek goddess of harmony and peace. Sappho 70.

Hector In Greek mythology, a prince of TROY who died in the Trojan War; husband of ANDROMACHE. Sappho 44i.

Helen In Greek mythology, the most beautiful woman in the world. The goddess APHRODITE helped Paris, a prince of TROY, to abduct her from her Greek husband, causing the Trojan War. Sappho 16i and 23.

Helicon A Greek mountain that was the mythological home of the MUSES. Epigram 6.

Hellas Ancient name for GREECE. Epigram 4.

Hellenistic Period Period of Mediterranean history between the death of Alexander the Great in 323 B.C.E. and the transition of Rome into an empire around 31 B.C.E.

Hera Queen of the Greek gods; the goddess of marriage and women's affairs. "Papyrus Sappho Obbink" and Sappho 17.

Hermes In Greek mythology, the messenger of the gods, and god of travelers, tricksters, and poets. Sappho 95 and 141.

Hermione In Greek mythology, the daughter of HELEN. Sappho 23.

Hermoclides A man mentioned by Sappho. His name means"son of Hermocles." Epigram 1.

Herodotus Fifth-century B.C.E. Greek historian.

Heroides Literally, "The Heroines," a collection of fifteen fictional letters from abandoned women written by OVID. All of the supposed letter writers but Sappho are characters from Greek and Roman mythology.

Hesperos Personification of the evening star. Sappho 104i.

Homer Eighth-century B.C.E. Greek epic poet, author of the *Iliad* and *Odyssey.* Epigram 8.

Homeric Hymns Collection of thirty-three hymns to the Greek gods composed in the seventh and sixth centuries B.C.E. Ancient writers commonly misattributed them to HOMER; their actual authors are unknown.

Hymen Another name for the god HYMENAEUS. Epigram 6.

Hymenaeus Greek god of marriage ceremonies and wedding nights. Sappho 111.

Idaeus In Greek mythology, a herald from the city of TROY. Sappho 44i.

Ilion Another name for TROY. Sappho 44i.

Ionia A region of western central ASIA MINOR, home to a group of Greek colonies. Sappho 98.

Irana A girl or woman mentioned by Sappho. Her name may mean "peace." Sappho 91 and 135.

Itys In Greek mythology, the son of Procne and her husband Tereus. After Tereus raped and imprisoned Procne's sister, Procne murdered Itys for revenge. The gods then turned the family into birds: Tereus became a hoopoe, Procne a swallow, and her sister a nightingale. *Heroides* 15.

Kerkylas According to ancient bibliographical sources, the husband of Sappho, who hailed from ANDROS.

Kleis According to ancient bibliographical sources, the daughter of Sappho. Sappho 98 and 132.

Larichus According to ancient bibliographical sources, the youngest of Sappho's three brothers, after CHARAXUS and EURYGIUS, and her favorite. "Papyrus Sappho Obbink."

Leda In Greek mythology, a mortal woman who was seduced or raped by ZEUS and bore HELEN. Because Zeus took the form of a swan, it was said that Helen was born from an egg. Sappho 166.

Lefkada An island off the western coast of the Greek mainland, location of the Cliffs of LEUCAS.

Lesbos A Greek island off the coast of ASIA MINOR, homeland of Sappho. Sappho 106; Epigram 9; *Heroides* 15.

Leto Minor Greek goddess, the mother of ARTEMIS and APOLLO. In one legend, the mortal NIOBE boasted that her fourteen children made her superior to Leto, and Artemis and Apollo slaughtered all of Niobe's children to punish her. Sappho 44ii, 99, and 142; Epigram 1.

Leucadia Another name for LEFKADA. *Heroides* 15.

Leucadian Sea Sea below the CLIFFS OF LEUCAS on LEFKADA. *Heroides* 15.

Leucas The Cliffs of Leucas are located on the coast of the island of LEFKADA, where Sappho supposedly jumped to her death. The cliffs were also home to a temple to APOLLO.

Lydia A kingdom in western ASIA MINOR which flourished during the twelfth to sixth centuries B.C.E. Sappho 16i, 39, 96, and 132.

Mars Roman name for the Greek god ARES. *Heroides* 15.

Medea In Greek mythology, a foreign sorceress who aided the hero Jason in his quest for the Golden Fleece. OVID wrote one of his *HEROIDES* from her point of view. Sappho 186.

Megara In Greek mythology, a princess of the city Thebes in GREECE, and first wife of the hero Heracles. In geography, a city on the coast of mainland GREECE. Sappho 68.

Meniscus A man mentioned in one epigram attributed to Sappho; nothing else is known about him. Epigram 3.

Methymna A city on the northern coast of LESBOS. *Heroides* 15.

Mica A girl or woman mentioned by Sappho; nothing else is known about her. Sappho 71.

Mimnermus Late seventh-century B.C.E. Greek lyric poet, known for his love poems and drinking songs.

Mitylene Alternate spelling of MYTILENE. Epigram 5.

Mygdonia A region of northeastern mainland GREECE. *Heroides* 15.

Mytilene A city on the southeastern coast of LESBOS, of which Sappho was a citizen. Sappho 98.

Moera Most likely an alternate spelling of Moero, a third-century B.C.E. Greek poet, one of the few Greek women whose writing survives. Epigram 7.

Mnasidika A girl or woman mentioned by Sappho; nothing else is known about her. Sappho 82.

Muses Nine Greek goddesses whose chief function was to inspire artists. Sappho 44ii, 55i, 58, 103i, 127, 128, 150, 187, and 214ii; Epigrams 4, 5, 6, and 9; *Heroides* 15.

Naiad In Greek mythology, a type of NYMPH who inhabited bodies of fresh water. *Heroides* 15.

Nausikaa In the *ODYSSEY*, a young princess who grants ODYSSEUS safe passage into her father's kingdom.

Nereids In Greek mythology, a group of fifty NYMPHS who inhabited the ocean. Sappho 5.

Niobe In Greek mythology, a mortal woman who boasted that her fourteen children made her superior to the immortal LETO, who had only two. Sappho 142.

Nisaia Ancient town just south of the Zagros mountain range in modern Iran. *Heroides* 15.

Nymph In Greek mythology, a nature spirit which took the form of a beautiful woman. Sappho 214i; *Heroides* 15.

Odysseus Mythological king of the Greek island Ithaca, who spent ten years attempting to return home to GREECE from TROY after the Trojan War.

Odyssey Epic poem composed by HOMER, which tells the story of ODYSSEUS' homeward journey.

Olympus Mythological mountain home of the Greek gods. The "lord of Olympus" is ZEUS. Sappho, "Papyrus Sappho Obbink" and 27.

Ovid Roman poet who lived from 43 B.C.E. to 17/18 C.E.; author of the *HEROIDES*.

Oxyrhynchus Archaeological site in northern Egypt, where over two-thirds of all surviving literary papyri have been discovered.

Pandion In Greek mythology, a king of ATHENS and father of Procne. See ITYS for more information on this myth. Sappho 135.

Panormos Ancient town on the northern coast of SICILY. Sappho 35.

Paphos An ancient city on the southwestern coast of CYPRUS; home to one of the most important temples to APHRODITE in the Greek world. Sappho 35.

Parian Marble Marble block found on the island of PAPHOS in the early seventeenth century, engraved with a timeline of ancient Greek history.

Parthenon Sacred storehouse in ATHENS dedicated to the goddess Athena.

Pegasus In Greek mythology, a winged horse who created the created the sacred spring of the MUSES when he struck Mount HELICON with his hoof. The Muses are not literally the daughters of Pegasus, but their homeland is associated with him. *Heroides* 15.

Pelagon A man mentioned in an epigram attributed to Sappho; nothing else is known about him. Epigram 3.

Pelasgians A pre-Greek people whom the Greeks viewed as barbaric and primitive. However, Roman authors use the words "Pelasgian" and "Greek" interchangeably. *Heroides* 15.

Penthilus Ruler of MYTILENE, whose family was known for its oppressive rule. Sappho 71.

Persephone Greek goddess of the Underworld, springtime, and rebirth; wife of HADES. Epigram 2.

Perseus Mythological hero best known for rescuing the princess ANDROMEDA (2) from a sea monster. *Heroides* 15.

Persia A region of modern-day Iran that was known in Sappho's time as a colorful and exotic place.

Persuasion (*Peitho* in Greek) Personification of persuasion as an attractive goddess, often associated or even conflated with the goddess APHRODITE. Sappho 96; Epigram 4.

Phaedra In Greek mythology, the sister of ARIADNE who married the hero Theseus and fell in love with her husband's son. OVID wrote one of his *HEROIDES* from her point of view.

Phaon Mythological ferryman, a favorite of APHRODITE; often associated with or even confused with ADONIS. *Heroides* 15.

Phocaea Ancient Greek city on the western coast of ASIA MINOR. Sappho 101.

Phoebe Roman name for the Greek goddess of the moon, Selene, who caused her mortal lover Endymion to sleep forever so that he would never age or die. *Heroides* 15.

Phoebus Alternate name for the Greek god APOLLO. The two names can also be used in conjunction. Sappho 44ii.

Phoenicia Ancient Semitic civilization that began in modern Israel. During Sappho's time, there were Phoenician settlements on the coast of North Africa, the Iberian Peninsula, Sardinia, and SICILY.

Phrygia Ancient kingdom in the central region of ASIA MINOR. During Sappho's time, Phyrigia became a province of LYDIA. Sappho 92.

Pieria A region of mainland GREECE associated with the MUSES, who were said to dwell near a sacred spring on Mount HELICON. Sappho 55 and 103i; Epigrams 4 and 6.

Plakos A mountain in ASIA MINOR near the town of THEBES. Sappho 44 i.

Pleiades Seven NYMPHS; daughters of the Titan Atlas and the nymph Pleione. They were companions of ARTEMIS, and later memorialized as a cluster of stars. Sappho 168i.

Polyanax A man mentioned by Sappho; possibly the patriarch of a family that rivaled hers. Sappho 99, 155, and 213ii.

Priam In Greek mythology, the last king of TROY and father of HECTOR. Sappho 44i.

Propertius First-century B.C.E. Roman elegist.

Pyrrha (1) Ancient city on the island of LESBOS. *Heroides* 15.

Pyrrha (2) See DEUCALION. *Heroides* 15.

Sardis Ancient capital of LYDIA in ASIA MINOR. Sappho 96 and 98.

Sauniadas A man mentioned in an epigram attributed to Sappho; nothing else is known about him. Epigram 1.

Sicania The central region of SICILY. *Heroides* 15.

Sicily A large island off the southern coast of Italy where Sappho reportedly lived during her exile from LESBOS. *Heroides* 15.

Sisters Refers to the FATES. *Heroides* 15.

Socrates Athenian philosopher who lived from c. 470 to 399 B.C.E.

Solon of Athens Early sixth-century B.C.E. Greek statesman and poet living in ATHENS.

Sparta An ancient city-state in southern GREECE, known for its military culture.

Thalía MUSE of comedy and idyllic poetry. *Heroides* 15.

Thebes A city in ASIA MINOR that HOMER identifies as the hometown of ANDROMACHE. Not to be confused with better-known cities of the same name in GREECE and Egypt. Sappho 44i.

Thyone In Greek mythology, a mortal woman from the city of Thebes in GREECE who was seduced by ZEUS and conceived DIONYSUS. Thyone was also called Semele. Sappho 17.

Tibullus First-century B.C.E. Roman elegiac poet.

Timas A woman mentioned in an epigram attributed to Sappho; nothing else is known about her. Epigram 2.

Tithonus Mortal lover of the goddess DAWN. In the *HOMERIC HYMN to APHRODITE*, the gods grant him immortality, but Dawn forgets to ask for his eternal youth. Sappho 58i.

Troy Ancient city on the coast of ASIA MINOR. In Greek mythology, the Greeks laid siege to Troy for ten years in order to reclaim HELEN. Sappho 16i, 17, and 44i.

Tyndareus Mythological king of SPARTA and husband of LEDA. His sons are Castor and Pollux. Sappho 68.

Typhoeus In Greek mythology, a gigantic monster whom ZEUS trapped under Mount AETNA. He was said to create storms or volcanic clouds with his hellish breath. *Heroides* 15.

Tyrtaeus Late seventh-century B.C.E. Greek poet from SPARTA.

Venus Roman name for the Greek goddess APHRODITE. *Heroides* 15.

Zeus Olympian ruler the Greek gods,. Sappho 1, "Papyrus Sappho Obbink," 17, 44ii, 53, 99, 103i, and 180.